Minorities in Medicine

From Receptive Passivity to Positive Action

1966–76

by

Charles E. Odegaard

Minorities in Medicine

From Receptive Passivity
to Positive Action 1966–76

by

Charles E. Odegaard

THE JOSIAH MACY, JR. FOUNDATION
One Rockefeller Plaza, New York, New York 10020

Manufactured by Port City Press, Baltimore, Maryland
Distributed by the Independent Publishers Group,
14 Vanderventer Avenue,
Port Washington, New York 11050

To Betty
Steadfast and Courageous Companion
in the Cross Fire

Foreword

When the Foundation's efforts began, we referred solely to "medicine," but we soon added "health professions"—for we were repeatedly reminded that a career ladder might begin with medicine as the focus and then shift to medical technology, nursing, pharmacy, dentistry, or the many other allied fields.

More than half of the black students now enrolled in medical school have attended or graduated from black colleges. Preparation for medicine in most of these colleges has not kept pace with new concepts in the sciences. From the beginning, therefore, the Foundation's major emphasis has been on expanding the pool of medical school candidates in the black colleges.

The Foundation's various initiatives have been based on developments in this field and are discussed in sequential order:

1. Support of a postbaccalaureate program, which included a summer school experience and a fifth year of college for minority college graduates to bring their scholastic records up to academic parity for entry to medical school. The students were recruited by a team led by the dean of an excellent small liberal arts college in the North and his wife.

2. The convening of a series of national and regional conferences to establish confidence and encourage cooperation and communication between the black colleges and the predominantly white medical schools. Presidents of the black colleges and their premedical advisors did not believe that the medical schools were sincere in their search for minority group students; and premedical advisors in particular were not familiar with the procedures and requirements for entering the study of medicine. On their part, medical school admissions officers were not acquainted with the faculties of the black colleges in their region or state, and some gave no more than lip service to black recruitment.

3. Grants to medical schools for special summer programs at the college level to strengthen the preparation of minorities, to support their recruitment, and to develop programs to encourage high school and college students to enter careers in the health professions.

4. A special effort to strengthen recruitment by Southern medical schools beginning in 1968. We were concerned that the best candidates

from the black colleges were being recruited by Northern medical schools.

5. At about this time, also, admissions officers in the predominantly white medical schools complained that their efforts were often thwarted because qualified graduates of black colleges were not receiving adequate preparation in those subjects that would ensure their acceptance or in the procedures necessary for entry into medical school. In 1971 and 1972 the Foundation therefore held two summer institutes on premedical advisory services for faculty members of black colleges and awarded a series of follow-up grants to strengthen the colleges' premedical advisory services.

6. The lack of role models of the same ethnic group on medical school faculties is seen as a negative factor by minority medical students. Thus in 1970 the Foundation established a faculty fellowship award program for minority groups as an incentive for their career development. This program was discontinued after three years, however, because we concluded that the funds used for the awards could be invested more fruitfully in other areas. Furthermore, we learned that many black faculty members were so burdened by their participation in special recruitment programs and in guidance and counseling activities that their advance up the career ladder was endangered.

We believe that the forecasts of special commissions, which led to undue optimism that the ratio of black doctors would reach the same level as that of blacks in the total population, were unrealistic. Enough qualified minority group applicants are simply not available. Furthermore, in the wave of emotion that followed the assassinations in 1968 of Martin Luther King, Jr., and Robert F. Kennedy, a number of medical schools admitted poorly prepared black students; the effect on both students and faculties was predictably traumatic. In addition, the anticipated levels of federal scholarship and loan support have never materialized, further thwarting hopes of enrolling more minority students. Another factor that may have diverted attention from this particular area of social justice is the unprecedented rise in the number of women entering American medical schools.

The Macy Foundation's present efforts are now focused on strengthening minority students' preparation for medical school, primarily through special programs for teachers of the biological sciences in black colleges.

After a ten-year commitment to increasing minorities in medicine, we decided that it would be appropriate to invite an experienced educator to appraise developments and to forecast future needs and opportunities.

Charles E. Odegaard, Ph.D., who had just left the presidency of the University of Washington after fifteen years of outstanding leadership, was uniquely qualified to undertake such a study. He has served on commissions and participated in studies on medicine and related fields. During his presidency, the University of Washington Medical School rose to a position of national eminence. Charles Odegaard's special commitment to expanding opportunities for minorities brought him to national attention as the defendant in the DeFunis case. It is pertinent that although the U.S. Supreme Court refused to rule on that case because DeFunis was already enrolled in law school, the court agreed in February 1977 to rule on a similar appeal by a medical school applicant in California who claims that he was denied admission because of reverse discrimination based on a quota system of the school.

Charles Odegaard's acceptance of our invitation was acclaimed by a variety of organizations active in minority programs. We believe that this report will not disappoint. Indeed, it will stand as a landmark study, and his findings will raise challenges that have implications for the entire structure of medical education and for all medical students.

A special word of thanks goes to Miss Maxine E. Bleich, Program Director of the Macy Foundation, whose overriding commitment during the past decade has been to minorities in medicine. She has steered Charles Odegaard's manuscript through the meticulous editorial process, which every landmark report deserves.

John Z. Bowers, M.D.
President
Josiah Macy, Jr., Foundation

Contents

Introduction

The reader of this report is entitled to know at the outset that it is not free of value judgments. It expresses some convictions as to goals for public policy and direction of social movement, and it addresses itself to what ought to be done to permit movement toward those goals.

It is fitting that this introduction is being written concurrent with the last events associated with the bicentennial commemoration of the birth of the American nation, for the lodestar guiding this study of minorities in medicine is the goal of equal opportunity for all citizens espoused in the doctrines of the founding fathers. Admittedly, at the beginning of the republic, the actual fell short of the ideal; but for over 200 years there has been substantial progress toward realization of the ideal—in comparison with many other nations. Thus, there is even more reason to continue striving for full realization of the ideal for *all* Americans.

Even as we accept the ideal as a goal, it is not always easy to determine how each of us may help to bring the actual closer to the ideal. I must admit that my own perception of what I could and should do within my sphere of personal influence has developed and changed over time.

Certain accidents of my own upbringing in Illinois early made me more aware of the existence of religious prejudice between Protestant and Catholic, and between Christian and Jew, and of the possibilities of discriminatory action by the dominant group. Living in New England as an undergraduate and graduate student from 1928 to 1937 provided ample additional opportunity to see the discriminatory possibilities stemming from virulent religious prejudice. When I began teaching at the University of Illinois in 1937, I found a steady stream of Jewish students from East Coast cities whose access to higher education in New England and the Middle Atlantic states was restricted and who had to come to public institutions in the Middle West for a greater opportunity for self-improvement.

This greater awareness of the impact of religious prejudice on the achievement of the American ideal unquestionably influenced the direction of my studies in history. My major focus became the intellectual and religious history of the Middle Ages, which set the stage for so much of the conflict in modern Western civilization induced by religious affiliations. As I began teaching, I found Protestants, Catholics, and

1

Jews, and even members of the clergy, in my classes. As they learned more of their respective histories, and especially of their common heritage, they tended to become more understanding of one another—even as their differences survived—and antipathy frequently was reduced. In my lifetime, surely, while religious prejudice and the possibilities for discriminatory actions inspired by it can still occur, we have seen a subsidence of the divisive effect of religious differences in our society and in the incidence of discriminatory actions against smaller groups attributable to religious prejudices.

This experience offers grounds for hope that in time discriminatory actions inspired by racial prejudice may also be mitigated so that as a nation we will come closer to achieving our ideal. The raising of my own awareness of the extent of racial prejudice and its discriminatory consequences to the level of an active concern had to await the prodding of the civil rights movement of the 1950s.

Shortly after coming to the University of Washington as president in 1958, I asked for a review of its existing policy about discrimination and its statements thereon. I found that the institution appeared to be among the more liberal in its stance, as attested by certain practices then identified as indicators of actual policy. For a decade it had been increasing the pressure on fraternities and sororities to remove religious and racial exclusionary clauses from their charters. There were no restrictions on assignments to residence halls by reason of religion, race, or color. In both the admissions and appointment process no information was solicited as to religion or race; and, a test case for the time, no photographs were included in the individuals' dossiers. Officers of the highly organized student government obviously included individuals from diverse religious backgrounds; and though the number of black students was visibly small, there were instances, if rare, of their election to student offices. The university, which appeared to me to be open to all qualified comers, was dedicated to a color-blind policy. There appeared to be little more needed than a reaffirmation of the existing policies on equality of opportunity issued in a university memorandum in February 1959 the preamble of which stated, "The University of Washington . . . affords equal opportunity without regard to race, creed, or color, to all persons, whether students, teachers, or members of administrative and service staffs."

In the next several years the only incident to trouble smooth waters on the campus with accusations of discriminatory action came in a charge not of racial but of anti-Semitic behavior in connection with an election to a student office. As president I quickly came under pressure to intervene immediately with paternal discipline. I refrained from such action, focusing attention instead on the fact that the student government had an elections commission composed of students empowered to judge such matters. The result was three weeks of agonizing by a group of students, charged with responsibility by their fellows, who had to face religious prejudice and its consequences. In bringing the incident to a generally satisfying conclusion they provided for themselves and for many other interested students a salutary learning experience.

Meanwhile the black community in Seattle had become increasingly activist, though it had not yet attacked the university. At commencement in June 1963 I was shaken out of my naïve confidence in the openness of the university and the adequacy of its "color-blind" policy. As the long line of graduates filed by, it dawned on me that despite the presence of a black community hardly two miles away and despite the talk about the expansion of opportunity for blacks in our society, there were remarkably few blacks among the graduates. I asked myself, since the university is presumably open to them, why were there so few? The regents had been seated beside me at the ceremony. Afterward, while we were changing from our academic gowns, I reported my impression. They confirmed it and shared my curiosity as to why we saw so few blacks. This was the beginning of a whole new learning experience about some of my fellow Americans with whom I had previously had very little association, a learning experience that is still going on.

I was gradually to learn how much really has to be done to open a predominantly white educational institution to a minority group and how much we must change our perceptions about the educational process in general, if it is to provide real equality of opportunity for minority persons who historically have been discriminated against by being excluded from full participation in American society and have received unequal treatment in educational opportunity. Learning about this special educational problem, particularly as it relates to actions at the university level, has been for me an unfolding of one new vista after another.

To help me begin this learning experience, I arranged in the fall term of 1963 to free a member of the faculty half-time to consult with members of the black community and with what proved to be a surprisingly small group of faculty expertly informed first about black minority communities and later about other minority communities.

In May 1965 I appointed a committee on special educational programs consisting of academic administrators and faculty to advise on the conduct of actual programs to encourage the entry of more minorities first into undergraduate education and later into the graduate programs. There is no need here to describe the subsequent steps in the development of special programs for minorities; they are by no means completed, nor has the need for them passed away. It is important only that the reader know that I am identified and myself identify with the idea that "business as usual" is not a sufficient response to the needs of educationally disadvantaged minority groups, if many of them truly are to have access to and take advantage of opportunity at the university level. There is still room for differences in judgment as to the wisdom of a given tactic, but I do wish the reader to know of my commitment to the goal that obviously colors this report, even as I have tried to be fair to all parties involved.

At least since 1966 the Josiah Macy, Jr. Foundation, under the presidency of John Z. Bowers, M.D., and I have been on a converging course. Within health and medicine, the area defined by its charter, it has been a pioneer in supporting programs intended to encourage the entry of more minorities into medicine. It has maintained its interest in this objective in the intervening years. Late in 1974 Dr. Bowers asked me to undertake a review of experience in the effort to introduce more minorities into the profession, a review not of Macy-supported projects as such but of the experience of the medical schools in general. This proposal fitted well with the interest I had developed, as here described. It gave me an opportunity to study the problem of education for minority groups with reference to a very important profession, entry to which is based on a long and arduous educational pathway. I was pleased to undertake this assignment, which has consumed most of my time in 1975 and 1976.

It remains to define which minorities are meant in this study. They should be distinguished in important particulars from other minorities who have been in the United States. Apart from the English-speaking settlers from Great Britain and Northern Ireland and their successors from this area, other immigrants have usually passed through the stage of being, in the face of a dominant English-speaking majority, minorities noticeably different in cultural characteristics, speaking either a foreign tongue or halting English.

The majority of these immigrants came to America as the promised land symbolized by the Statue of Liberty, a land that offered opportunity to those willing to work for it and to improve their lot and status. In some cases they also came to escape religious or political persecution in their homeland. In any case they came by choice, intending to become Americans. With varying rates of speed over the generations, different ethnic groups, transplanted by their own volition, have passed by means of cultural assimilation from the status of a separate ethnic minority to the majority American citizenry.

One variable that has tended to influence the speed of assimilation of immigrant groups has been the change in the availability and cost of transportation. In the days of sail the possibility that an immigrant could return for visits to the mother country was restricted by the length of the voyage, the availability of space, and the high cost. Renewing ties to the "old country" was little likely; and enduring commitment to, and contentment with, the ways of the new country could emerge quickly. With the development of steamships and the increase in trade toward the end of the nineteenth century and the beginning of the twentieth, the cost and the duration of transoceanic travel were reduced. Hence, immigrants in the later streams now heavily from central, eastern, and southern Europe, if not deterred by political difficulties, could afford to revisit their homeland and so refresh their ties with its people, language, and culture. They would thus be influenced to retain even longer their distinctively different way of life, often in "ethnic neighborhoods." In time, however, the later generations became absorbed into the mainstream of the American majority.

Changes in the immigration laws after World War I sharply limited the massive migrations to this country, with the resulting attrition of the older ethnic neighborhoods, as the descendants of the original occupants merged culturally into the majority. The relaxation of immigration laws since the end of World War II has seen the revival of some of this old pattern of immigrant movement, especially from the Orient, in the appearance of Koreans, Filipinos, and recently Vietnamese, and of groups from South and Central America.

The American commitment to public education and the relative ease of access to higher education have, of course, provided a social elevator that ambitious immigrants, and especially their offspring, could use to equip themselves culturally and occupationally to enter middle-class American society. By now, in all probability most members of the American majority are descended from one or another ancestor who at some point in our history was perceived as a member of an ethnic minority. However, these descendants, having finally made their way into the dominant middle class, can now, if they wish, sentimentally engage in activities reminiscent of their ethnic origins without losing the sense of being really Americans.

Even though the gates of the United States are much narrower than they were before the 1920s, they are not closed. Since World War II political circumstances elsewhere have encouraged the acceptance of political refugees from a wide variety of classes in their home countries. Old patterns of assimilation of immigrant groups can be expected to repeat themselves in various ways in the case of minority groups composed of these more recent immigrants.

The minorities in the United States with which this report is concerned differ in significant particulars, though in different ways, from the usual immigrant groups who have ultimately come to perceive themselves and to be perceived as members of the American majority. They are the American Indians, Black Americans, Mexican Americans, and Mainland Puerto Ricans.

The American Indians are not, in any meaningful sense of the word, immigrants to this land. It is rather, the immigrants and their descendants who physically overpowered the Indians, took most of their lands, confined their holdings largely to sharply limited reservations, and placed them under the conqueror's law in a distinctive subordinate status as wards of the United States. The American Indians already had their own cultural traditions. They did not abandon their home country and elect to come here. They were already here, pursuing their own way of life. Descendants still adhere in varying degrees to a separatist way. The special provisions administered by the Bureau of Indian Affairs help to confirm their separated status within American society. American Indians offer few points of comparison with the usual ethnic minority immigrants.

The same is true for Black Americans, who came from Africa, not of their own accord but as slaves brought unwillingly to be sold into slavery here under whites. Even though the abolition of legal slavery was guaranteed by the result of the Civil War, legally imposed disabilities continued, justified by the "separate but equal" doctrine. Legal and customary separation from whites, and the inevitable, long-imposed alienation from the dominant white majority, sharply distinguishes the experience of Black Americans from that of the usual immigrant minorities for whom access to the dominant majority was open.

The Mexican American minority is usually viewed by the dominant majority as an immigrant group composed of individuals who entered the United States of their own accord, in sizeable numbers, some of them illegally. Hence, if they or their offspring have acquired American citizenship, it is up to them to Americanize themselves as other immigrants have done. The Mexican Americans, on the contrary, tend to view their presence within the United States in a different perspective. They consider Texas, New Mexico, Arizona, even the southern parts of Colorado and Utah, and California, as regions of their homeland seized by conquest by newcomers, the Anglos. In these areas the more recently arrived Mexican Americans see the Spanish language and Mexican customs and ways with which they identify surviving among Mexican Americans long resident in the area. The southern border as the white majority perceives it is simply not regarded as a border by some Mexican Americans, who often have families on both sides of this line; this encourages and legitimates in their minds free travel across the "border." This sense of Mexican American solidarity is obviously expressed in terms of the effort to preserve the Spanish language and *la raza,* Mexican American culture. On the basis of the Treaty of Guadalupe-Hidalgo of 1848, many Mexican Americans also believe that there is a legally approved basis for retention of their culture within a fully American context. These attitudes clearly separate the Mexican American "immigrants," to use the Anglo reference, from other ethnic groups whose movement into the mainstream of the American majority was favored by a very different set of attitudes affecting their presence in the United States.

The absence of an oceanic or sea border, the contiguity of territory with Mexico, and the resulting relative ease and cheapness of travel by automobile between Mexican American settlements within the United States and Mexico further encourage retention of the old cultural and linguistic ties that separate Mexican Americans from the dominant English-speaking majority.

The situation with reference to Mainland Puerto Ricans is somewhat similar. Their presence in large ethnic neighborhoods primarily in a few cities along the northeastern seaboard is a phenomenon of the past generation. Here again we are not dealing with immigrants in the usual sense. The United States occupied Puerto Rico as a consequence of the Spanish-American War, falling heir to Spain as a colonial power. Thus American hegemony reached out and around a people of different language and culture, while allowing their separate linguistic and cultural character to endure. A special situation results when Puerto Ricans move to the mainland United States. The tendency toward separatism is reinforced by their continuing contact with Puerto Rico, only a short distance by air from the northeastern settlements of Puerto Ricans.

American Indians, Black Americans, Mexican Americans, and Puerto Ricans, for differing reasons, thus constitute special cases of ethnic minorities separated not only by substantially different attitudes and experiences but by continued educational disadvantages. These minorities also share a disadvantage resulting from the circumstances of their particular racial mixture. More of their members are visibly distinguishable from the dominant majority by their darker skin and certain related physical features. The prejudice of whites against people with darker skins has a long history. It is expressed in negative attitudes that encourage the preservation of this psychological distance between these four ethnic groups and whites that their cultural differences had already created. Even efforts by members of these minorities to merge with the majority have been deterred by this color prejudice.

Each of these four minority groups has been separated and alienated within the United States. For them the conventional educational process, as an instrument for acculturation and for opening careers to talented individuals, has not been working well. Among other things, these groups have been persistently underrepresented in the numbers of their members who have completed medical education and become physicians. It is for this reason that these four minority groups have recently become the objects of special attention, as described in this report.

I wish to emphasize that, as will be noted in detail later, the number of these long-underrepresented minorities in medical schools has substantially increased since consistent data began to be collected annually in 1968–69; by 1975–76 there has been roughly a fivefold increase in the total enrollment and in the first-year enrollment of minority students. (The figures for 1976–77 minority enrollment show a very slight overall increase.) Most of this increase, which was brought about by increased enrollment in predominantly white medical schools, would not have occurred had it not been for changes made within these schools. This fact should be acknowledged, and the accomplishments of the responsible administrators and faculty members recognized. It is, however, the burden of this report that the task is not finished and that there is more to do. In advocating and seeking additional ways to bring about change to improve the representation of these minorities in medicine, it is comforting to see that salutary changes have indeed occurred. This awareness can encourage hope that still more can be accomplished.

*   *   *

Among many who have expressed interest in this study and have been helpful to me, it remains to acknowledge a few who assumed special burdens in reading my manuscript and in making critical comments or suggestions. These are, from the staff of the Association of American Medical Colleges a former colleague, August G. Swanson, and Dario Prieto; from the University of Washington School of Medicine, Charles W. Bodemer, Morgan N. Jackson, M. Roy Schwarz, and Robert L. VanCitters; from the College of Education, James A. Banks, Robert G. Cope, Samuel E. Kelly, James A. Vasquez, and Donald T. Williams; and from the School of Business Administration, Borje O. Saxberg. I am especially indebted to John Z. Bowers and Maxine E. Bleich of the Josiah Macy, Jr. Foundation, not only for their review of my manuscript but for advice and assistance of many kinds during the conduct of this study.

The responsibility, however, for the final content of this report, including its sins of omission or commission, rests squarely on my shoulders.

I am indebted for the subtitle of this report to Dr. Roy K. Jarecky of the University of Kentucky.

Finally I must express my appreciation to my assistant, Mrs. Pat Killingsworth, for data collection and the dogged determination and care she gave to producing a clear, accurate, and neat manuscript, despite my penchant for emending emendations.

C.E.O.

December 1976

We must not overlook the possibility that the very hangover from some of the disabilities of Negro Americans may allow for a resurgence of prejudice and prejudicial action. If, as seems the case, a good many more Negroes could get into medical schools than now qualify, it is easy for people to say, "I told you so!" and to fall back into old practices. One of our most serious questions of social policy is, then, this: Shall we merely try hard to act as if race had never existed? Or shall we undertake to remove by special action the handicaps left over from our long history of racial discrimination? Some Americans will argue that the first course is better; it would be the old-fashioned, laissez-faire, liberal course. Others will argue that, even at the risk of what might be called counter-discrimination, we must reduce the handicaps, provided we do not reward mediocrity.*

---

* Everett Cherrington Hughes, April 1958, in his introduction to Dietrich C. Reitzes, *Negroes and Medicine* (Cambridge: Harvard University Press, 1958): p. xxxi.

Chapter 1
The Basis of This Report

In order to assess the experience of medical schools during the last decade in their deliberate endeavors to increase the numbers of minorities in medicine, I have reviewed the literature on the subject, which consists mostly of journal articles describing programs developed in particular schools. Through the courtesy of Professor John S. Wellington, M.D., of the University of California at San Francisco, I was privileged to see in manuscript draft the only general review of programs for minorities in medicine contained in the "Report of Survey and Evaluation of Equal Educational Opportunity in Health Profession Schools" undertaken by him and Pilar Gyorffy, Ph.D., under a contract with the Department of Health, Education and Welfare.[1] Their report is based largely on the results of a lengthy questionnaire sent to the deans of predominantly white professional schools of dentistry, medicine, optometry, osteopathy, pharmacy, podiatry, public health, and veterinary medicine. In the case of medicine the questionnaire was sent in April 1974 to the deans of 112 medical schools (all of the then accredited United States medical schools except for the two predominantly black medical schools, Howard and Meharry);[2] responses were received from 89 schools. Each dean was asked to answer the questionnaire with reference to the 1972–73 academic year. Each of the responding schools was asked to indicate the year in which it first became significantly involved in equal educational opportunity efforts; the percentage of schools so reporting for each year are as follows:

Earliest Year of Involvement	Percent
1968 or before	34
1969	24
1970	15
1971	15
1972	7
1973	5
	100

Source: Wellington and Gyorffy, Table II

11

Thus, almost 90 percent of the 89 responding schools became involved in what they regarded as a significant way in the four years from 1968 to 1971.

Since medical schools had so recently been asked to complete an extensive survey by the questionnaire method and because of Dr. Wellington's generous offer to make the result of his survey available to me, I considered it unnecessary and inappropriate—indeed unmerciful —to impose another questionnaire upon the medical schools.

I had decided, in any case, to make visits to a number of medical schools. During 1975 and the first months of 1976, I visited, in addition to the Howard University College of Medicine in Washington, D.C., the Meharry Medical College in Nashville, Tennessee, and the Biomedical Program at City College of New York City, the following forty medical schools (a 36 percent sample of the 112 predominantly white medical schools then in full operation):

University of Alabama School of Medicine, Birmingham, Alabama
University of Arizona College of Medicine, Tucson, Arizona
University of California (Davis) School of Medicine, Davis, California
University of California (Irvine) California College of Medicine, Irvine, California
University of California (San Diego) School of Medicine, San Diego, California
University of California (San Francisco) School of Medicine, San Francisco, California
University of Southern California School of Medicine, Los Angeles, California
Stanford University School of Medicine, Stanford, California
University of Colorado School of Medicine, Denver, Colorado
Yale University School of Medicine, New Haven, Connecticut
University of Florida College of Medicine, Gainesville, Florida (including Florida State University and Florida A & M, Tallahassee, Florida)
University of Chicago Pritzker School of Medicine, Chicago, Illinois
University of Illinois College of Medicine, Chicago, Illinois
University of Kansas Medical Center School of Medicine, Kansas City, Kansas
University of Kentucky College of Medicine, Lexington, Kentucky
Tulane University School of Medicine, New Orleans, Louisiana
University of Michigan Medical School, Ann Arbor, Michigan
Wayne State University School of Medicine, Detroit, Michigan

Michigan State University College of Human Medicine, East Lansing, Michigan
University of Minnesota-Duluth, School of Medicine, Duluth, Minnesota
University of Minnesota Medical School-Minneapolis, Minneapolis, Minnesota
University of Mississippi School of Medicine, Jackson, Mississippi
Saint Louis University School of Medicine, St. Louis, Missouri
Washington University School of Medicine, St. Louis, Missouri
University of New Mexico School of Medicine, Albuquerque, New Mexico
Albert Einstein College of Medicine of Yeshiva University, New York, New York
Columbia University College of Physicians and Surgeons, New York, New York
Duke University School of Medicine, Durham, North Carolina
University of North Carolina School of Medicine, Chapel Hill, North Carolina
University of North Dakota School of Medicine, Grand Forks, North Dakota
University of Oklahoma College of Medicine, Oklahoma City, Oklahoma
Pennsylvania State University College of Medicine, Hershey, Pennsylvania
University of Pennsylvania School of Medicine, Philadelphia, Pennsylvania
Temple University School of Medicine, Philadelphia, Pennsylvania
Vanderbilt University School of Medicine, Nashville, Tennessee
Baylor College of Medicine, Houston, Texas
University of Texas Southwestern Medical School, Dallas, Texas
University of Texas Health Science Center at San Antonio Medical School, San Antonio, Texas
University of Utah College of Medicine, Salt Lake City, Utah
University of Washington School of Medicine, Seattle, Washington

These institutions are distributed geographically from North to South and East to West and are located in metropolitan areas and in smaller cities. They include public and private institutions. Some are long-established and of greater prestige; others are more recently established and of lesser reputation. Some are "innovative" in educational philosophy and practice, and others are more conservative or orthodox. They vary also in the immediacy of their exposure to nearby communities peopled by one or another of the four minority groups: Black

American, American Indian, Mexican American, and Mainland Puerto Rican. The schools with the smallest total minority enrollment in 1975–76 had 9 students, that with the largest, 117; there were 7 schools with total minority enrollments in the 30s, 7 in the 40s, and 7 in the 50s. Ten schools had minority enrollments running from 60 to 117, and 10 from 9 to 29. While no claim is made that the schools visited constitute a scientifically selected sample, they are sufficient in number and varied enough in character to provide a reasonable base for generalizing about the medical schools' experience in minority programs.

My usual procedure was to initiate a prospective visit by telephone conversation with the dean of the school or with a close associate known to have direct responsibility for minority student matters. Invariably I received a welcoming response, and after a mutually convenient date for a visit had been established, I confirmed the matter in a letter, which also generally summarized briefly the objectives of my visit:

> It may be helpful to you and others to have this background information. I have been asked to develop a report and recommendations for general public distribution to anyone interested. The report will be based on a review of experiences in medical schools of the United States in their efforts to increase the number of minority students enrolled in medical schools and moving into the medical profession . . . .
>
> It is in connection with this study that I am visiting your medical school. I am hoping to have interviews with a selection of persons: administrators, faculty, students, persons of minority and majority, if possible. I am interested in comments about your institution's experience in all aspects related to the problems of recruiting applicants from schools and colleges to the admitting process and to the handling of students actually enrolled in medical schools. I would like to know what effect the presence of more minority students, who have been encouraged to enroll, has had on faculty, students, and curriculum. It is not my intent to quote publicly individuals or to comment on named institutions. I do hope for candid comments from individuals based on their perceptions of their own experience.

It should be noted that I hoped particularly for candor from those interviewed, whatever their status or ethnic origin. As an encouragement to fuller and more open expression on the part of administrators, faculty, and students, I foreclosed the possibility of attributing comments to named individuals. For the same reason, after much debate with myself over the utility of a tape recorder for reference and for checking accuracy, I abandoned the idea in favor of taking occasional notes as less inhibiting to more relaxed and open expression. I can never know what the harvest would have been had I used a recording device. What I do know is that I had many conversations about a subject that inevitably and unhappily is fraught with tension for all participants; conversations, however, in which individuals of all ranks and colors were frequently remarkably candid about their individual fears and troubles, about their hopes and disappointments, and about their own actions and doubts—to a degree that often amazed me. This level of confidence shown me by so many of these interviewees as revealed by their candor has placed upon me a heavy responsibility to report as accurately, fairly, and judiciously as possible.

Since 1968 the Association of American Medical Colleges (AAMC) has been actively involved in programs supportive of minorities in medicine, including the collection of much useful data. Its staff officers, John A. D. Cooper, M.D., President; August G. Swanson, M.D., Director of the Department of Academic Affairs; Davis G. Johnson, Ph.D., Director of the Division of Student Studies; and Dario Prieto, Director of the Office of Minority Affairs, have been particularly informative about AAMC activities and helpful with relevant data.

As useful personal background for this investigation, I brought the information about medical education, the medical profession, and health care gained from a succession of intensive short courses beginning in the 1960s that included my membership in the National Advisory Health Council, the AMA Citizens Commission on Graduate Medical Education (the Millis Commission), the National Advisory Commission on Health Manpower (1967), National Institutes of Health (NIH) council assignments, and more recently the Study Commission on Pharmacy. I have also drawn on the still broader framework provided by experience as a professor of medieval history (a perspective more pertinent to the functioning of the health guilds, so it seems to me, than some might think!); as assistant for the humanities to the graduate dean (University of Illinois); as dean of arts and sciences in a faculty that, in addition to teaching its own graduates, was heavily involved in "servicing" students enrolled for degrees under other faculties (University of Michigan); and as president of a large university with an active health sciences program as well as a substantial involvement in an effort to open the doors of its many faculties to minority students (University of Washington).

This report is based on the complex of information derived from the sources indicated.

Beginning about 1968 a mounting wave of enthusiasm to bring more minority students into the study of medicine swept through the country. All of the 89 predominantly white medical schools that responded to the Wellington questionnaire claim that by 1972–73 they had become significantly involved in equal educational opportunity efforts. The range and depth of this involvement could and does vary enormously. Interested and imaginative administrators and faculty of particular medical schools inserted one or another special program intended to attract or support minority students on the pathway to medical careers, sometimes with costs covered by funds immediately available to schools, sometimes with the help of foundation or government grants. The list of types of helpful programs for minorities grew rapidly after 1968, aided undoubtedly by the participation of interested persons who shared their experience in conferences sponsored by foundations and the AAMC and in meetings of the AAMC Group on Student Affairs. The converted who emerged from these meetings had a substantial influence, but obtained different levels of response from the medical schools. Some schools quickly developed multifaceted programs involving major alterations of established ways and substantial expenditures, even of their "own" funds, in addition to foundation and federal grants. Some schools made a limited number of changes, and still others undertook very few modifications. Hence, some program items believed to be helpful to the progress of minority students reappear in many schools, while others are found in fewer instances.

In the ensuing chapters I will turn first to a brief sketch of the rise of concern to increase the number of students of minority origin in medical schools, followed by a chapter on the actual numbers involved up to 1975–76. I will then take note of two possible deterrents to positive action, legal difficulties and the need for money. It is only fair, then, to note those particular circumstances of their prior history that made—and continue to make—the effort to recruit minorities for education as physicians a major challenge for change in medical schools. The implementation of such a change required, and still requires, a very high level of commitment from the faculty of a medical school. Further positive change to keep the program of action moving ahead in many medical schools depends upon refurbishing their commitment to positive action on behalf of minorities. There will then follow a description of special programs developed to recruit minorities into medical schools and to improve their chances of graduating.

NOTES

1. John S. Wellington and Pilar Gyorffy, "Report of Survey and Evaluation of Equal Educational Opportunity in Health Profession Schools," unpublished mimeographed draft (San Francisco: University of California, 1975).

2. Two additional medical schools intended to serve minority students are in the course of being established. Morehouse College, a predominantly black undergraduate institution in Atlanta, Georgia, is adding to its program a medical school that will offer the first two years of instruction in medicine; for instruction in clinical medicine its students transfer to the medical schools of Howard, Meharry, and Emory. An American Indian School of Medicine is now planned. Though the primary initiative has come from the Navajo Health Authority, the planners intend to educate American Indian and Alaska Native students as primary physicians who will practice on Indian reservations and in other medically deprived areas. The first two years of the curriculum are to be provided through contract with Northern Arizona University at Flagstaff; the later clinical instruction will be based primarily at the Indian Health Service Hospital at Shiprock, New Mexico.

Chapter 2
From Receptive Passivity to Positive Action

At the instigation of Dr. Franklin C. McLean, founder of the National Medical Fellowships, Incorporated, which had been organized to provide financial assistance to blacks for education and training in medicine, Dietrich C. Reitzes undertook a study in the mid-1950s, the results of which were published in 1958 as *Negroes and Medicine*. The study presented data on the number and proportion of blacks in medical school, their distribution among predominantly white and predominantly black medical schools, the number of applications and acceptances, and their relative standing on the Medical College Admission Test (MCAT) in various types of schools. It described and analyzed the medical care provided by and for blacks in fourteen urban areas across the nation; and then, based on comparisons of the situations in these communities, it developed generalizations about those factors that encouraged or discouraged integration in the medical care provided for blacks and between black physicians and whites.

In his introduction, Dr. McLean summarized certain conclusions from this study, as follows:

> The United States today is confronted with a serious shortage of Negro physicians which affects not only the medical care of Negroes but the health of the entire country. This shortage of Negro physicians is demonstrated by the fact that while Negroes made up 10% of the total population in 1950, Negro physicians constituted only 2.2% of all physicians. And while the percentage increase of Negro physicians between 1940 and 1950 was 14.2%, the Negro population increased by 17% during the same period. Thus, while there has been a continuous increase in absolute numbers of Negro physicians, there has been no progress toward improving these numbers in relation to the increasing need.[1]

An increase in the 2.2 percentage of black physicians among all physicians could come, of course, only from a relative increase in the number of blacks enrolled in medical schools and graduating from them. Dr. McLean continued:

> The number of Negro medical students, however, is still inadequate from two perspectives. First, the proportion of Negro medical stu-

18

dents to white medical students has not increased since 1947–48 and does not even approach the proportions of Negroes to whites in the total population. This is so because since 1947 there has been a significant increase in the total number of medical students in the United States. Between 1947–48 and 1955–56 Negro students increased by 29.4%, from 588 to 761; during the same period however, the number of all medical students increased by 25.9% from 22,739 to 28,639. Second, from the perspective of the need for Negro physicians, there is no indication that the Negroes in medical schools today will alleviate the shortage of Negro physicians since the proportion of Negro students to all students (2.6%) is only slightly greater than the proportion of Negro physicians to all physicians (2.2%).[2]

Despite its implications for efforts to increase the proportion of black medical school graduates, the Reitzes study fell for almost a decade on deaf ears. The total black enrollment in medical schools rose by only ten students, from 761 in 1955–56 (the last year included in the Reitzes study) to 771 in 1961–62, only to fall back substantially to 715 in 1963–64. While the two predominantly black medical schools, Howard and Meharry, increased their black enrollment slightly over this eight-year period, all other medical schools, the predominantly white medical schools, had a noticeably reduced black enrollment, from 236 to 173. Hence, the percentage of black medical students enrolled in predominantly white schools fell from its high-water mark of 31.0 percent in 1955–56 to 24.2 percent in 1963–64.[3]

Thus despite the removal of all legal barriers to admission of blacks to medical schools following the Supreme Court decision of 1954 in *Brown* v. *Board of Education,* and the increase in the number of predominantly white schools to which blacks were admitted, the number actually enrolled in white medical schools had decreased from 1955–56 to 1963–64. Howard and Meharry were still carrying three-quarters of the black medical school enrollment, with only one-quarter distributed in the predominantly white medical schools then in existence.

In 1958 Dr. McLean indicated that a basic problem in increasing the number of blacks in medical schools was their preparation. Data in the Reitzes study showed that, generally speaking, the mean MCAT aptitude test scores of blacks from black colleges and applicants to the two black medical colleges were lower than those of all applicants to medical schools. He attributed these differences to cultural factors, such as family structure and the educational opportunities of blacks in American society.[4]

The National Medical Fellowships, Incorporated, which had sponsored the study, continued its program of grants-in-aid to medical students and shared its interest in increasing minority representation in medicine with the black medical community, in particular with the National Medical Association. In November 1965 the NMA held a symposium on talent recruitment at its annual meeting. At this conference, Edward Warner Brice, Director of the Adult Education Branch of the United States Office of Education, pointed out that disadvantages existed not only for blacks but also for Puerto Ricans, migrant whites, American Indians, and Spanish Americans.[5] In 1965 a group of black professionals in New York held a conference to discuss ways to encourage junior high school students to head toward medical education and made ten recommendations:[6]

1. Better advising in high school and college;
2. Better sources of information for designated faculty of traditionally Black institutions about requirements for admission to medical school, the admissions process, medical school curriculum, attitudes toward Black students, and opportunities for Black physicians;
3. Strengthening of teaching of premedical sciences and English at the traditionally Black institutions;
4. Establishment of special premedical programs by Howard and Meharry;
5. Non-academic support for the special problems of Black students in traditionally white medical schools;
6. Elastic preclinical programs to provide additional experience before matriculation for intellectually competent students;
7. Establishment of 2-year medical schools in close association with predominantly Black colleges and universities, to prepare students for admission into 4-year schools at the 3rd-year level;
8. Strong allied health profession training in the above 2-year schools—the multi-track system;
9. Additional special programs to strengthen educational preparation at the college level for Black students with strong potential for medicine; and
10. Special programs to attract Black women into medicine.

Most of these recommendations were subsequently implemented to some degree—but only after the white majority had bestirred itself and after whites had become more actively involved in helping minorities enter medicine in larger numbers.

In September 1966 the Josiah Macy, Jr. Foundation, in a pioneering move initiated by its president, Dr. John Z. Bowers, took steps to help blacks improve their preparation for admission to medical schools by establishing the Post-Baccalaureate Premedical Fellowship Program under the administration of William E. Cadbury, Jr. For the first year, eleven black college seniors were selected to attend a special summer instructional program held in 1967 at Haverford College; they then spent the academic year 1967–68 at Haverford, Bryn Mawr, Swarthmore, Oberlin, Kalamazoo, or Pomona College in courses intended to strengthen their academic preparation for medical school. In 1968–69 the eleven black students were enrolled in medical colleges, eight at predominantly white schools; each was further assisted by a $2,500 grant-in-aid from the Macy Foundation.

In October 1966 the attention of AAMC members was directed to the underrepresentation of women and blacks in medicine by the report "Minorities, Manpower, and Medicine," presented to the Group on Student Affairs at the association's annual meeting in San Francisco by Edwin B. Hutchins of the AAMC staff.[7] This underrepresentation posed serious problems and has received increased attention in the following decade. The cultural circumstances affecting the underrepresented groups, however, are dissimilar; and this report concerns only the status of black and other ethnic minorities, and not sexist discrimination as such.

The Macy Foundation encouraged further discussion of methods for increasing the number of blacks in medicine by sponsoring a series of conferences, beginning with "Negroes for Medicine" in June 1967 and followed by two on related themes in February and June 1968. To these conferences were invited administrators and faculty from medical schools and black colleges, and representatives from philanthropic foundations. These and subsequent conferences helped arouse concern for increasing the number of blacks in medical schools and for discovering ways to increase the number of black applicants regarded as qualified for admission.

As word of these matters spread, administrators and faculty became receptive to change. They began to propose various kinds of actions intended to encourage and support interest in the development of methods for preparing blacks for entry into medical education. In 1968 the Macy Foundation began giving financial aid through medical schools

to projects for the improvement of preparation for medical education in
the traditionally black colleges; to projects for the strengthening of communication, cooperation, and confidence between the traditionally black
colleges and the medical schools; and to projects for the identification
and academic support of minority group high school and college students
with a potential interest in a medical career. Extending its activities to
the medical school years, the foundation also aided compensatory educational programs in the medical schools to bring minority group candidates up to academic parity.[8]

The assassination of Dr. Martin Luther King, Jr., in April 1968,
spurred liberally oriented administrators and faculty in medical schools
to greater action to recruit and admit minorities. It also aroused the
social activism of white students in many of the predominantly white
medical schools. Their initiative undoubtedly helped induce other faculty
and administrators of these schools to increase their interest in encouraging and accepting black applicants from across the nation.

Meanwhile the seed planted by the Hutchins report in 1966 began
to take root within the national organization of medical schools. The
Executive Council of the AAMC had approved the recommendation of
its Committee on Student Affairs that it cosponsor the Macy conferences
in 1968. The first, held in Atlanta in February, centered on "Preparation for Medical Education in the Traditionally Negro College:
Recruitment—Guidance—Curriculum"; and the second, held four
months later in Fort Lauderdale, dealt with "Liberal Arts Education and
Admission to Medical School." The purpose of the latter was to bring
together for discussions premedical advisors from colleges in the Deep
South and medical school admission officers.

At the annual meeting of the AAMC in November 1968, Dr. Herman
Branson of Central State University reported to the Group on Student
Affairs on these conferences, on the need for massive scholarship funds
for minority students aiming for medicine, and on the need to examine
the MCAT as a selection device.[9] Dr. Roy K. Jarecky of the University
of Kentucky reported on medical school efforts to increase minorities
in medicine, presenting the results of a May 1968 survey of such efforts
and providing illustrative details on a number of specific projects to
increase the number of minorities. Citing related efforts at the undergraduate level, he encouraged every member institution to reevaluate its
efforts in this area. He concluded his report by saying, "In general,
medical schools are beginning to change their stance from one of receptive passivity to positive action with respect to recruiting and preparing

RMG [Racial Minority Groups] students for medicine." Noting that this effort required cooperation among all medical schools, he recommended that the AAMC Group on Student Affairs establish a program to identify, recruit, and if possible, place minority groups in medical schools.[10]

Continuity of attention by the AAMC to minorities in medicine was assured by actions in 1969. In that year the AAMC obtained grants from the U.S. Office of Economic Opportunity for the establishment of an Office of Minority Affairs within the AAMC staff, which from 1969 to 1973 expended $1.5 million on some fifty programs supportive of minority students in medicine. It also received financial help for a significant venture from the Alfred P. Sloan Foundation, which since 1959 had been contributing annually to National Medical Fellowships, Incorporated, for the support of ten black medical students. In 1968 it began to increase the amount of support to provide for more students, and in 1969 it provided financial support to the AAMC for its task force established to formulate a report, "Expanding Educational Opportunities in Medicine for Blacks and Other Minority Students." This report was submitted to the Inter-Association Committee representing the American Medical Association, the National Medical Association, the American Hospital Association, and the AAMC itself. Published on April 22, 1970, the report indicated that the percentage of black physicians (2.2 percent) remained the same as that reported twelve years earlier, though the percentage of blacks in the total population was 11–12 percent.[11]

It will be noted that in 1969 the AAMC had established an Office for Minority Affairs and that the task force refers to expanding educational opportunities for "Blacks and Other Minorities."

In his report to the AAMC in 1966, Hutchins stated that a workable definition of a minority group had been offered by Louis Wirth as follows:

A group of people who, because of their physical or cultural characteristics, are singled out from the others in the society in which they live for differential and unequal treatment . . . .

Minority group status carries with it the exclusion from full participation in the life of the society. . . . While minorities more often than not stand in a relationship of conflict with the dominant group, it is their nonparticipation in the life of the larger society that more particularly marks them as a minority people and perpetuates their status as such.[12]

In his report Hutchins had applied this concept only to blacks. Recognizing the minority group status of other ethnic groups within the United States, the Macy Foundation in 1968 provided support to medical schools for programs intended to facilitate the entry into medicine not only of blacks but also of American Indians, Mexican Americans, and Puerto Ricans.

Similarly, the AAMC also included in its minority enrollment reports beginning with 1968–69 these four groups and also the category Oriental (later American Oriental). Beginning with the publication of the 1973–74 data, the category American Oriental was deleted from the table called "Selected Minority Group Enrollment," which still included Black American, American Indian, Mexican American, and Mainland Puerto Rican.[13]

More recently the four "selected minorities" have appeared under the heading "Underrepresented Minorities"; American Oriental was included under the heading "Other U.S. Minorities," and the category "Other" listed a small number of U.S. citizens from various countries overseas. The separation of American Orientals from the four groups is explained as "not underrepresented in medicine."[14] Most recently the category Cuban American has been joined with Oriental American under the heading "Other U.S. Minorities."[15]

The category American Oriental poses in and of itself certain problems, since persons from so many countries tend to be included. At the same time there may be substantial variations in the socioeconomic, educational, and linguistic status of individuals within a given group that is ultimately of the same national origin. Time itself brings changes in the way of additions, as for example the recent influx of Vietnamese refugees. Whatever the problems of categorizing for purposes of statistics, the medical schools are becoming more adept at recognizing educationally and culturally disadvantaged groups that have a resultant record of lower participation in the life of the larger society and, in particular, in medical education and practice. In most parts of the country this awareness is now extending to the recognition of rural white populations as underrepresented minorities.

To return to the AAMC Task Force report of 1970 with its focus on minorities as Black Americans, American Indians, Mexican Americans, and Mainland Puerto Ricans, it provided a broad framework for thinking about increasing educational opportunities for minority students in medicine and encouragement for a wide range of potential supportive actions.[16] The task force proposed as a short-term goal that medical schools increase the representation of minorities in the M.D. degree programs to 1,800 entering minority students by 1975–76, estimated to be 11.9 percent of the total medical school enrollment. While it was not explicitly stated, it must have been the assumption that this increase in enrollment would come essentially in minority admissions to the predominantly white medical schools.

Recognizing the importance of financial aid to students, both at the undergraduate and at the medical school level, the task force made a variety of specific recommendations with regard to short- and long-term financing of medical students. Aware of the need to provide factual and personal information to minority students about career opportunities in the health professions for motivational purposes, the task force recommended a network of regional centers to provide an interface between minority communities and colleges and medical schools. It recommended that the AAMC seek the necessary funding to expand its Office for Minority Affairs as a source of information for prospective medical students, counselors and advisors, and academic institutions. Then the task force presented in diagrammatic form an analysis of the educational pathway that students must follow in high school in order to become successively qualified college applicants, college students, qualified medical applicants, and M.D. recipients. The task force also identified at successive points along the pathway the major reasons for student exit from the educational flow toward the M.D. degree, indicating appropriate action to help the student to remain with the flow. These action elements were identified as the student himself, student groups, the educational institutions, minority community groups, the practicing profession, government, financial institutions, and foundations.[17]

On December 16, 1970, as further recognition of the goals expressed in the Task Force Report, the Executive Council of the AAMC made the following statement:

> The AAMC and its constituent members are directing earnest attention and effort toward the goal of increasing minority opportunities in medical service, teaching, and research. A detailed description of these goals (including the short-term objective of 12 percent minority medical entrants by 1975–76) is contained in the "Report of the AAMC Task Force to the Inter-Association Committee on Expanding Educational Opportunities in Medicine for Blacks and Other Minority Students" that was approved by the AAMC Executive Council on May 7, 1970.
>
> Medical Schools, working with cooperating preprofessional colleges, are urged to help increase minority student awareness of the

opportunities for professional education and the specific preparation necessary for medical school. Minority students, thus motivated, prepared, and recruited, should be provided encouragement to complete their course of study.

In order to provide the most conducive educational milieu, medical schools are urged to identify a faculty member or administrator who can be specifically charged with responsibility for minority student affairs. This individual should work closely with the AAMC Group on Student Affairs (GSA) and should represent the medical school in GSA minority affairs activities. An individual from a minority group may be particularly effective in this position.

In developing new and modifying existing educational programs, medical school faculties should be aware that minority students, while not always as well prepared in the traditional sciences basic to medicine, bring to the profession special talents and views which are unique and needed. Educational programming for all medical students should be sufficiently flexible to allow individual rates of progress and individualized special instruction. With such programming, the opportunity for minority student success will be maximized.

The AAMC-AMA Liaison Committee on Medical Education is strongly encouraged to review critically the degree of individual opportunity provided in medical school curricula. The Liaison Committee is also urged to include in its membership (and on its accreditation teams where possible) individuals with special knowledge and experience in the education of minority group students.

Financial assistance for minority students must be maximized and medical schools are urged to pursue actively the expansion of minority student support funds at the local, state, and federal levels. The Association is making known to the American public and to the Federal Government these needs for increased financial aid for minority students.

In support of minority programs the AAMC undertook to provide useful services. To the enrollment data gathered from all medical schools, it added statistics on the number of selected minorities admitted to the first year of medical school and the total enrollment in medical schools in each academic year beginning in 1968–69.[18]

To make generally available to premedical advisors, premedical students, and potential applicants to medical schools information on each medical school's program to recruit, admit, and retain minority students, the AAMC published *Minority Student Opportunities in United States*

Medical Schools 1969–70. Minority enrollment statistics for each school were added to the 1970–71 and 1971–72 versions. An updated version was published as *Minority Student Opportunities in United States Medical Schools 1975–76.* Meanwhile the AAMC, beginning with the 1973–74 edition of its annual bulletin, *Medical School Admission Requirements,* added a regular chapter entitled "Information for Minority Group Students," which in addition to brief general information provided the latest information for each medical school on its minority enrollment; the number of minorities in its basic science faculty, clinical faculty, and administration; and the name of its contact person.

The AAMC also initiated as a regular service for minority students, beginning with applicants for entry in 1970–71, the Medical Minority Applicant Registry (Med-MAR). Students are invited to participate voluntarily in Med-MAR by identifying themselves as belonging to a minority group, either on a questionnaire completed when they take the MCAT or by contacting the AAMC directly. This program provides the opportunity for any medical school applicant belonging to a minority group to have basic biographical information circulated to all United States medical schools at no cost. By this means medical school admission offices have been able to identify easily minority students and then to initiate contact with potential applicants, particularly in their own region of the country.

In the 1970s the AAMC sponsored, with financial assistance from the Grant Foundation and federal funds, a number of national and regional workshops to discuss ways in which schools can strengthen their programs in the areas of recruitment, selection, and retention. Particular attention has been given by its Office of Minority Affairs to improving selection systems for students whose backgrounds are dissimilar from those of the essentially white middle-class applicants who constituted the bulk of the applicant pool in the 1950s and 1960s. In 1973 the Simulated Minority Admissions Exercise was introduced in regional workshops in an effort to develop a system that could be used by medical school admissions committees to regularize their identification of those specific variables (other than the standard cognitive measures, aptitude test scores, and prior academic grades) that are pertinent to the selection of nontraditional, minority students who are more likely to succeed in medical school.

Because enough has happened to stimulate the development of special programs for encouraging the entry into medical schools of underrepresented minorities, assessment of these efforts is warranted. The next step is a résumé of the changing numbers of minority students involved in medical education.

NOTES

1. Dietrich C. Reitzes, *Negroes and Medicine* (Cambridge, Massachusetts: Harvard University Press, 1958): p. xxvii.

2. *Ibid.*, p. xxii.

3. The figures for black enrollments in 1961–62 and 1963–64 are in Edwin B. Hutchins, Judith B. Reitman, and Dorothy Klaub, "Minorities, Manpower, and Medicine," *Journal of Medical Education* 42 (September 1967): 809–821.

4. Reitzes, p. xxiii (see note 1).

5. Edward W. Brice, "The Conservation of Human Resources," *Journal of the National Medical Association* 57 (November 1965): 441–443.

6. James L. Curtis, "A Plan to Promote Professional Careers for Negroes," *Journal of the National Medical Association* 57 (November 1965): 168–172.

7. Hutchins *et al.*, 809–821 (see note 3).

8. Josiah Macy, Jr. Foundation, *Annual Report for the Year 1968* (New York: Josiah Macy, Jr. Foundation, 1968).

9. Association of American Medical Colleges, "The Seventy-Ninth Annual Meeting," *Journal of Medical Education* 44 (May 1969): 381–382, 444.

10. Roy K. Jarecky, "Medical School Efforts to Increase Minority Representation in Medicine," *Journal of Medical Education* 44 (October 1969): 912–918.

11. Association of American Medical Colleges Task Force, *Report to the Inter-Association Committee on Expanding Educational Opportunities in Medicine for Blacks and Other Minority Students* (Washington, D.C.: Association of American Medical Colleges, 22 April 1970).

12. Hutchins *et al.*, 809 (see note 3).

13. Association of American Medical Colleges, *Medical School Admission Requirements 1975–76, United States and Canada*, 25th ed. (Washington, D.C.: Association of American Medical Colleges, 1975): p. 54.

14. W. F. Dubé and Davis G. Johnson, "Study of U.S. Medical School Applicants, 1973–74," *Journal of Medical Education* 50 (November 1975): 1015–1032.

15. W. F. Dubé, "Datagram: Medical Student Enrollment, 1971–72 Through 1975–76," *Journal of Medical Education* 51 (February 1976): 144–146.

16. AAMC, *Task Force Report 1970* (see note 11).

17. Bernard W. Nelson, Richard A. Bird, and Gilbert M. Rodgers, "Educational Pathway Analysis for the Study of Minority Representation in Medical School," *Journal of Medical Education* 46 (September 1971): 745–748.

18. AAMC, *Admission Requirements 1975–76* (see note 13).

Chapter 3
Minority Enrollment in Medical Schools

It will be remembered that the Reitzes study drew attention to the fact that in 1950 black physicians constituted only 2.2 percent of the nation's physicians, when blacks constituted 10 percent of the population, and that this shortage could be overcome only by increasing the number of black medical students. Twenty years later, however, in 1970, the number of blacks employed in medicine was still 2.2 percent, still far below the proportions of blacks in the U.S. population which, according to the 1970 census, had increased to 11 percent.[1]

Whereas the earlier efforts by blacks to increase the number of minorities in medicine seem to have aroused little concern and action in the predominantly white medical schools, when these black efforts were joined by white initiatives beginning in 1966, the message was destined finally to reach more receptive ears in more places—and the mountain began to move. The idea that blacks and other underrepresented minorities should be encouraged and helped by members of the majority to enter the pathway for medical education was gradually backed by administrators, faculty, and students in various medical schools, by association and foundation officers, and by federal government programs. Their backing began to change the numbers of minorities enrolled in medical schools as revealed in the consistent data collected by the AAMC beginning with 1968–69. The changes in the number of Black Americans, American Indians, Mexican Americans, and Mainland Puerto Ricans in American medical schools, both as to number and as to percentage of total enrollment for first-year as well as total enrollment, are shown for 1968–69 through 1975–76 in Tables 1 and 2.

The Black American first-year enrollment in medical schools in 1968–69 was 266, of which 133, or 50 percent, were enrolled at the predominantly black medical schools, Howard and Meharry. Of the total black enrollment in medical schools that year, however, 63 percent were at Howard and Meharry. Presumably the predominantly white schools in the immediately preceding years must have admitted even smaller numbers of black students than were admitted in 1968–69. The predominantly white schools continued to open their doors to more black students; and by 1975–76, 1,036 Black Americans were admitted to

TABLE 1

Selected Minority Group Enrollment in First-Year Classes in U.S. Medical Schools (1968–75)

Year	Black American * Number Enrolled	% of Total Enrollment	American Indian Number Enrolled	% of Total Enrollment	Mexican American Number Enrolled	% of Total Enrollment	Mainland Puerto Rican Number Enrolled	% of Total Enrollment	Total Selected Minority Group Number Enrolled	% of Total Enrollment	Total First-Year Enrollment
1968–69	266	2.7	3	0.03	20	0.2	3	0.03	292	2.9	9,863
1969–70	440	4.2	7	0.1	44	0.4	10	0.1	501	4.8	10,422
1970–71	697	6.1	11	0.1	73	0.6	27	0.2	808	7.1	11,348
1971–72	882	7.1	23	0.2	118	1.0	40	0.3	1,063	8.5	12,361
1972–73	957	7.0	34	0.3	137	1.0	44	0.3	1,172	8.6	13,677
1973–74	1,023	7.5	44	0.3	174	1.2	56	0.4	1,297	9.1	14,124
1974–75	1,106	7.5	71	0.5	227	1.5	69	0.5	1,473	10.1	14,763
1975–76	1,036	6.8	60	0.4	224	1.5	71	0.5	1,391	9.1	15,295

* Black Americans at Howard and Meharry medical schools accounted for 120 of these 1969–70 freshmen and 195 of these 1974–75 freshmen.

Source: AAMC enrollment data

TABLE 2

Selected Minority Group Total Enrollment in U.S. Medical Schools (1968–75)

Year	Black American* Number Enrolled	Black American* % of Total Enrollment	American Indian Number Enrolled	American Indian % of Total Enrollment	Mexican American Number Enrolled	Mexican American % of Total Enrollment	Mainland Puerto Rican Number Enrolled	Mainland Puerto Rican % of Total Enrollment	Total Selected Minority Group Number Enrolled	Total Selected Minority Group % of Total Enrollment	Total Enrollment
1968–69	783	2.2	9	0.02	59	0.16	3	0.01	854	2.4	35,830
1969–70	1,042	2.8	18	**	92	0.2	26	0.07	1,178	3.1	37,690
1970–71	1,509	3.8	18	**	148	0.4	48	0.1	1,723	4.3	40,238
1971–72	2,055	4.7	42	0.1	252	0.6	76	0.2	2,425	5.5	43,650
1972–73	2,582	5.5	69	0.2	361	0.8	90	0.2	3,102	6.5	47,366
1973–74	3,045	6.0	97	0.2	496	1.0	123	0.2	3,761	7.4	50,751
1974–75	3,355	6.3	159	0.3	638	1.2	172	0.3	4,324	8.1	53,554
1975–76	3,456	6.2	172	0.3	699	1.3	197	0.4	4.524	8.1	55,818

* Black Americans at Howard and Meharry medical schools accounted for 496 of these 1969–70 enrollees and 695 of these 1974–75 enrollees.

** Less than 0.1 percent.

Source: AAMC enrollment data

the first year of medical schools. Of these, despite some increases in the size of entering classes at Howard and Meharry, the percentage in the first-year classes of these two schools had declined from 50 percent in 1968–69 to 19 percent in 1975–76. Clearly the major arena for an increase in the number of places for Black Americans has been in predominantly white medical schools.

From 1968–69 to 1974–75 the total first-year medical school enrollment increased by one-half (from 9,863 to 14,763). During the same period, Black American first-year enrollment increased slightly over four times, to 1,106. The largest gains came in the first four years from 1968–69 to 1971–72, with smaller increases in the three years from 1972–73 to 1974–75. From a high of 1,106 in 1974–75 there was a decline to 1,036 in 1975–76. As a percentage of total enrollment, Black Americans increased in three notable jumps from 2.7 percent in 1968–69, to 4.2 percent in 1969–70, to 7.1 percent in 1971–72. Despite smaller but steady increases in actual numbers of first-year Black American medical school enrollment in 1972–73, 1973–74, and 1974–75, the Black American percentage of enrollment remained at or slightly above 7 percent, because these were years during which the total first-year enrollment continued to expand due to the opening of new medical schools and the expansion of existing schools.

The decline in Black American first-year enrollment, from the 1974–75 level of 1,106 to 1,036 in 1975–76, brought the percentage of Black Americans among all first-year enrollments to 6.8 percent. Possible causes of this subsidence will be discussed later, but it should not be overlooked that the latest number enrolled is still almost four times above the 1968–69 level.

By far the largest minority group underrepresented in medicine is the Black American group, which numbers, according to the 1970 census, 22,549,815 or 11.1 percent of the United States population. American birth or parentage was used as the identifier for another group, Spanish Origin Americans, also often referred to as "Spanish Surnamed"; but this category includes individuals from subgroups of substantially diverse cultural backgrounds, levels of education, and social classes. The more discernible subgroups easily recognized as underrepresented are the Mexican Americans, numbering 4,532,435 or 2.2 percent of the United States population, concentrated largely in rural but now also in urban areas in the Southwest and West and beginning to spread eastward and northward; and the Mainland Puerto Ricans, numbering 1,429,396 or 0.7 percent of the United States population, concentrated largely in urban areas along the northeastern seaboard. The smallest underrepresented minority is that of Native Americans, numbering 798,119 or 0.4 percent of the United States population; 96 percent of these are American Indians, the remainder being mostly Eskimo, and a small number of Aleuts. It should be noted that it is generally believed that undercounting of minorities in the census exceeds the undercounting of whites.[2]

Unlike Black Americans, who have benefited from the existence for many years of the two predominantly black medical colleges, the other underrepresented minorities have not had medical schools directed specifically toward them as a constituency. Especially given their geographical distribution, they are particularly dependent for medical education upon admission to the predominantly white schools.

The pattern of enrollment increases for first-year Mexican American medical students is much like that for the Black Americans, with steady increases from 20 in 1968–69 to 227 in 1974–75, followed by a slight drop to 224 in 1975–76. This represents an elevenfold increase, as compared with a fourfold increase for Black Americans. Mexican Americans, however, have among physicians an even lower representation than that of blacks. The percentage of total first-year enrollment has gone from 0.2 percent in 1968–69 to 1.5 percent in 1975–76, still short of the 2.2 percent represented by Mexican Americans within the U.S. population.

The numbers for American Indians and Mainland Puerto Ricans are somewhat similar. In 1968–69 there were enrolled in the first-year medical class three persons identified as associated with each of these two groups, in each case 0.03 percent of the total first-year enrollment. By 1974–75 in the case of American Indians, and by 1975–76 for Mainland Puerto Ricans, their number had increased almost 24 times.

In 1975–76 the first-year American Indian enrollment subsided from 71 to 60. This is still a twentyfold increase over the 1968–69 level and brings the percentage of total first-year enrollment to 0.4 percent, a figure that corresponds with the 1970 census percentage of Native Americans within the total population.

It is also possible to view from another perspective the results of the increase in participation of underrepresented minorities in medical education since the initiatives in 1966. If one were to postulate as a goal the attainment of a percentage of first-year enrollment equal to the percentage of each minority within the total population, then one could say that in the 1975–76 first-year enrollment the goal had been obtained to the following degree: American Indian 100 percent, Mainland Puerto Rican 71 percent, Mexican American 68 percent, Black American 61 percent. Things in 1975–76 are not where they were in 1966, or 1958, or 1950:

there has been progress. And we should appreciate the constructive effort of those who have contributed since 1966 to actions that have brought American ideals closer to realization. But there are no grounds for complacency. Smaller increases, for the most part beginning with 1972–73, were followed by some subsidence in the numbers of new entries by minorities into the first year of medical school in 1975–76. These results certainly indicate that the forward surge initiated in the late 1960s has stopped and raise questions as to the maintenance of the present level of minority enrollment. For the large numbers of minorities the numbers involved in 1975–76 still reflect a level well below any proportional representation—and that only in the first year of medical education.

Most students enrolled in the 1975–76 first-year class still must complete three years of medical school before receiving the M.D. degree and must then spend an average of four years in postgraduate education before they will be prepared to begin independent practice, a course that brings them essentially to 1982 as the first year of fully responsible medical practice. Without further increases in the number of minorities enrolled in medical schools, it will be a matter of decades before the number of minority physicians in practice can approximate the proportion of these minorities to the total population.

How well do minority students who *have* been admitted to the medical schools fare? What are their retention rates and their rate of progress? The most general report of this matter completed to date is the cooperative study of the Student National Medical Association (SNMA) and the AAMC published in July 1975 by Davis G. Johnson, Vernon C. Smith, Jr., and Stephen L. Tarnoff.[3] The authors were able to learn the retention and promotion status of the 1970 and 1971 matriculants at the end of their first year of medical school. Their findings are shown in Table 3. By way of explanation they note:

> The attrition categories include those individuals who are believed to have irrevocably exited from the medical educational system. This may be because of outright dismissal for either academic or nonacademic (disciplinary) reasons, or the student may have left of his or her own accord. The retention categories include those students retained in the medical education pathway, even if their progress may not be "regular." In addition to the vast majority of students promoted with their class, retainees also include students taking a leave of absence, repeating a year, or doing work on a Ph.D. or on a special research project. The "other" category

TABLE 3

Percentage of 1970 and 1971 Medical School Matriculants by Race Who Were in Various Categories of Academic Status at End of First Year of Medical School *

Status of Medical Student	Caucasian		Black American		American Indian		Mexican American	Puerto Rican ****	All Individuals **	
	1970 (5,799)***	1971 (8,943)	1970 (388)	1971 (546)	1970 (20)	1971 (39)	1971 (82)	1971 (108)	1970 (10,187)	1971 (11,904)
Attrition										
Dismissal, academic	.3	.5	2.6	4.4	5.0	.0	.0	.0	.6	.8
Left, other reasons	1.2	1.5	1.5	2.4	5.0	.0	1.2	1.9	1.3	1.6
Total	1.5	2.0	4.1	6.8	10.0	.0	1.2	1.9	1.9	2.4
Retention										
Leave of absence	.2	.5	.8	.9	.0	.0	1.2	.0	.3	.6
Repeating all or part of year	.6	.6	16.5	9.7	.0	5.1	4.9	1.9	1.5	1.5
Promoted with class	97.3	95.8	77.8	80.8	90.0	94.9	92.7	96.3	95.8	94.5
Total	98.1	96.9	95.1	91.4	90.0	100.0	98.8	98.2	97.6	96.6
Other	.4	1.1	.8	1.8	0.0	0.0	0.0	0.0	1.5	1.0

* No data available for Mexican Americans or Puerto Ricans for the 1970 entering class.
** Includes "unknown" and "other" racial designations.
*** Figures in parentheses are the total number of individuals about whom retention and promotion information was available at the time study was conducted.
**** Includes both mainland and island Puerto Ricans.

Source: Davis G. Johnson, Vernon C. Smith, Jr., and Stephen L. Tarnoff, SNMA–AAMC study, *Journal of Medical Education* 50 (July 1975): 754.

comprises a very small number of individuals whose status did not fit clearly into the attrition or retention groupings.

The most encouraging fact to emerge in the analysis of the retention/attrition data was that all the racial groups entering in 1970 and 1971 had retention figures higher than 91 percent at the end of their first year in medical school. Compared with other graduate and professional schools, this is very favorable. Moreover, it should dispel the rumor of exceptionally high attrition among minority students.

For the two classes studied, black students had slightly lower retention rates than did whites or most of the other minorities. For the 1970 and 1971 entering classes, the retention rates for blacks were 95 percent and 91 percent respectively, as compared with 98 percent and 97 percent for white students. These rates for blacks are similar to the national rates of a decade ago before the applicant pool was expanded and before maximum efforts were made to improve retention rates. . . .

Although differences in total attrition by race are not very sizable, greater disparities exist regarding immediate promotion from the first to the second year class. Black medical students had a lower than average immediate promotion rate, which means that more blacks will take an extra year to graduate than will students from other groups. The immediate promotion rate for blacks was approximately 80 percent for the classes in this study. This compares with about 96 percent for white students and the low to middle 90s for the other minority groups. It should be noted, however, that the number of students in the "other" minority groups is so small that the findings are of less validity than for the whites and blacks.

While these promotion figures indicate that some minority students, particularly blacks, are encountering difficulty in medical school, the results should not be interpreted too negatively. A closer look at the statistics reveals that the overwhelming majority of students who are not promoted on schedule are still retained in the educational pathway and are actively pursuing the M.D. degree.[4]

The information obtained in this study concerning retention after the first year of minority students admitted in 1970–71 and 1971–72 has been supplemented recently by data from the AMA regarding the retention of minority students in three subsequent classes. It provides the number and percentage retained after three years for those admitted in 1972–73, after two years for those admitted in 1973–74, and after one year for those admitted in 1974–75, as shown in Table 4.[5]

TABLE 4

Students Admitted 1972–73 Through 1974–75 and Still in Medical School or Graduated, June 1975

	Admitted 1972–73 Number	Retained June 1975	%	Admitted 1973–74 Number	Retained June 1975	%	Admitted 1974–75 Number	Retained June 1975	%
Black American	838	729	87	908	790	87	934	886	95
American Indian	30	27	90	37	31	84	63	62	98
Mexican American	140	134	96	167	157	94	203	198	97
Mainland Puerto Rican	37	35	95	48	47	98	60	59	98
All other students	12,045	11,751	98	12,393	12,066	97	12,892	12,750	99

Source: AMA data, *Journal of the American Medical Association* 234 (December 1975) : 1339, Table 14.
Copyright 1975, American Medical Association.

37

TABLE 5

Retention After the First Year of Minority Students Admitted in 1971–72
and in 1974–75

	Admitted 1971–72 * Retained June 1972 %	Admitted 1974–75 ** Retained June 1975 %
Black American	91.4	95
American Indian	100	98
Mexican American	98.8	97
Mainland Puerto Rican	98.2	98

Source: * Table 3
          ** Table 4

Because of the small numbers involved, the validity of statistical comparisons for Mainland Puerto Ricans and American Indians may be in doubt. The retention rate for Mainland Puerto Ricans remains high, at the 95 percent level at the end of the third year and at the 98 percent level at the end of the second and first years. For American Indians the pattern is more erratic, going from 90 percent at the end of three years, to 84 percent at the end of two years, to 98 percent at the end of one year.

Larger numbers are involved for Mexican Americans, and their retention level is far more consistent and averages are higher, from 96 percent after three years, to 94 percent after two years, to 97 percent after one year. For Black Americans the retention rate dipped somewhat lower to 87 percent after three years and 87 percent after two years, and then rose to 95 percent after one year. These figures for minority students may be compared with those for all other students, essentially whites, which run 98 percent after three years, 97 percent after two years, and 99 percent after one year.

Available data shown in Table 5 permit a comparison in retention after one year between the classes admitted in 1971–72 and in 1974–75.

The retention rate for Black Americans in the latter year is higher, in the mid-90 percent, and those for the other minorities are in the high 90 percent, close to the retention rate for nonminority students.

The AMA data on students repeating the academic year 1974–75 are shown in Table 6.[6]

Comparison of these data with those in Table 3 shows that medical students were promoted with their class at the end of their first year in the following percentages:

Year Admitted	Black Americans (%)	American Indians (%)	Mexican Americans (%)	Mainland Puerto Ricans (%)	All Others (%)
1971–72	80.3	94.9	92.7	96.3	——
1974–75	85.6	97.2	86.1	90.0	98.8

For the largest group, Black Americans, the percentage promoted at the end of the year improved noticeably from 80.8 percent to 85.6 percent. For the smaller group, Mexican Americans, the percentage promoted declined to a level comparable with that of Black Americans. For the still smaller groups of American Indians and Mainland Puerto Ricans, the figure remains in the 90 percent range. It can be noted from Table 6 that the percentages of Black Americans and Mexican Americans in 1974–75 who were at any class level beyond the first year and were required to repeat after their first-year class fell substantially below the level of the first-year class.

TABLE 6

Students Repeating the Academic Year 1974–75

	First-Year Class			All Other Classes		
	Enrolled Total	Repeating Number	%	Enrolled Total	Repeating Number	%
Black American	1,117	161	14.4	2,279	136	6.0
American Indian	72	2	2.8	89	7	7.9
Mexican American	231	32	13.9	407	33	8.1
Mainland Puerto Rican	71	7	9.9	97	7	7.2
All other students	13,472	162	1.2	36,239	229	0.6

Source: AMA data, *Journal of the American Medical Association* 234 (December 1975): 1339, Table 15. Copyright 1975, American Medical Association.

With regard to this matter of repeating, the AMA report notes:

Many of the "repeaters" are not repeating the first year, but rather following a decelerated program. An increasing number of schools have a flexible program that allows the student an opportunity to take the first-year courses over a longer period of time. These data suggest that the medical schools are making a continuing effort to ensure that their graduates, without regard to racial origin, will meet acceptable standards of competence. In enrolling a group of students known to be educationally disadvantaged, the medical schools have clearly chosen to provide these students with an opportunity to complete studies, rather than either lower standards or to drop a large proportion of these students from school.[7]

To recapitulate, this summary of the general statistical data available shows that minority students admitted in generally mounting numbers in the last eight years have presented more problems in the way of retention in the medical school program than have nonminority students. More minority than nonminority students leave either because of academic dismissal or for other reasons, and the rate of advance of minorities through the regular course of instruction is retarded more than that for nonminority students. But the basic point should not be overlooked that the flow of minority students through medical schools has increased noticeably. During the decade 1955–64 the number of Black Americans receiving M.D. degrees had remained fairly constant at about 166 a year. In 1970 the number was still 165 (2.0 percent of all degree recipients that year), the initiatives of the late 1960s not yet having influenced the graduating class of 1970. By 1973, however, the number of Black American graduates doubled to 341 (3.3 percent of the graduates that year). By 1975 the number had almost doubled again to 638 (5.0 percent of the graduating class).

For the other minorities, the actual number of graduates and the percentage of all graduates had also increased, as shown below: [8]

MINORITY M.D. GRADUATES

Year	Black American Number	%	Mexican American Number	%	American Indian Number	%	Mainland Puerto Rican Number	%
1970	165	2.0	10	0.1	4	0.05	9	0.1
1973	341	3.3	39	0.4	8	0.08	10	0.1
1975	638	5.0	110	0.9	22	0.2	28	0.2

The numbers of minorities both in medical schools and as graduated M.D.s are now different; they are larger than they were a decade ago. From 1955 to 1970, the number of black doctors had remained relatively constant, but in the five years from 1970 to 1975, it increased 3.9 times. For the other underrepresented minorities the number of graduated M.D.s increased from 1970 to 1975 as follows: Mexican American, 11 times; American Indians, 5.5 times; Mainland Puerto Ricans, 3 times.

The opportunity for minorities in medical education has definitely been improved almost entirely because in predominantly white medical schools there occurred, as Jarecky described it, a change of stance from one of receptive passivity to positive action with respect to recruiting and preparing minority group students. As late as 1963–64 the predominantly white schools had slightly less than one-quarter (24.2 percent) of the total black enrollment.[9] Figures available for first-year matriculants at medical schools show that the removal of legal barriers against blacks, followed by white initiatives evident from 1966, had had some effect by 1968–69, when first-year black enrollment in the predominantly white medical schools had risen to 50 percent of the total first-year black enrollment. In the next three years the predominantly white schools (as shown in Table 7) increased their share to almost 80 percent of the total first-year black enrollment, and during the last four years they have continued their share at the 80 percent level, or slightly higher.

As already noted, however, there has recently been a leveling and even a small subsidence in the first-year minority enrollments. It may be that in the first years after 1968 the numbers of minority individuals motivated to apply to medical school and judged qualified for admission was enlarged by the inclusion of a number of somewhat older individuals for whom entry into predominantly white medical schools previously might have seemed hopeless. This backlog may have been largely eliminated over a five- or six-year period, so that fewer such persons would be

TABLE 7

Number of First-Year Black Students in U.S. Medical Schools

Year	Howard and Meharry	Predominantly White Schools	Total	Percentage of Total in Predominantly White Schools
1968–69	133	133	266	50
1969–70	120	320	440	72.7
1970–71	170	527	697	75.6
1971–72	188	693	881	78.7
1972–73	196	761	957	79.5
1973–74	192	827	1,019	81.2
1974–75	195	911	1,106	82.4
1975–76	197	839	1,036	81.0

Source: AAMC enrollment figures

available for the pool of applicants. In more recent years, also, more opportunities have arisen for minorities to enter educational programs preparatory to advanced professional careers other than medicine, such as law, academic teaching, and business.

Despite the recent improvement in the contributions of predominantly white medical schools to minority students' education, these schools still have a substantial distance to go to raise the participation of minorities in medical education to a level proportional to their numbers in the American population.

NOTES

1. *Minorities and Women in Health Fields,* United States Department of Health, Education and Welfare, Publication No. (HRA) 75–22, May 1974 (Washington, D.C.: U.S. Government Printing Office, 1974): p. 7.

2. *Minority Health Chart Book,* American Public Health Association Report for 102nd Annual Meeting (Washington, D.C.: United States Public Health Service/Department of Health, Education, and Welfare, October 1974): pp. 1–2.

3. Davis G. Johnson, Vernon C. Smith, Jr., and Stephen L. Tarnoff, "Recruitment and Progress of Minority Medical School Entrants 1970–72," *Journal of Medical Education* 50 (July 1975): 713–755.

4. *Ibid.,* p. 738.

5. "Medical Education in the United States 1974–75, 75th Annual Report," *Journal of the American Medical Association* 234 (December 1975): 1339.

6. *Ibid.,* p. 1339.

7. *Ibid.,* p. 1339.

8. "Medical Education in the United States 1972–73, *Journal of the American Medical Association* 226 (November 1973): 913; *ibid.,* 234 (1975): 1339.

9. Hutchins *et al.,* "Minorities, Manpower, and Medicine," 815 (see note 3, Chapter 2).

Chapter 4
Special Programs for Minorities: Legally Permissible Or Not?

The slowdown in increases in the number of first-year minority medical students beginning in 1972–73, and the decrease in their numbers in the 1975–76 entering class, are very disturbing to those who have advocated the replacement of the earlier stance of receptive passivity with one of positive action by medical schools, since they do not see the desired goal yet reached. Obviously there is a value judgment here, a social value that fueled the surge of activity on behalf of minorities in the predominantly white medical schools in the past decade. This value was succinctly expressed in 1965 by Edward Warner Brice, Director, Adult Education Branch, U.S. Office of Education. Referring to disadvantaged minorities in a speech to the National Medical Association's Symposium on Talent Recruitment, he said:

> We cannot afford, as a nation, to limit the promises of democracy to only a part of the people. We owe equal opportunity for educational achievement to all our citizens so that each citizen, in turn, may bear his fair share of the responsiblities of democracy.[1]

In the first presentation to the AAMC of the subject of minorities in medicine as a problem for it, Hutchins in 1966 called attention to Gunnar Myrdal's *An American Dilemma* and stated:

> The dilemma lies not in the relations between the dominant group in America and the Negro minority but within the dominant group itself. The discrepancy that exists between the stated values of the equalitarian American creed and the actual behaviors employed in relations with the Negro American is sufficiently painful to present the dominant group member with a dilemma that is still far from being completely resolved. In a very real sense, the Negro Problem is a severe test of whether American democracy will remain a viable system for human interaction.

The lack of participation of blacks in medicine in particular was then viewed as a problem that Hutchins placed upon the shoulders of administrators of American medical education.[2]

The AAMC Task Force Report of April 1970 in a sense accepted this challenge and expressed the value motivating its recommendations as follows:

The long-term goal is to achieve equality of opportunity by reducing or eliminating inequitable barriers and constraints to access to this profession which have resulted in a representation of racial minorities in the medical profession much less than their representation in the U.S. population.[3]

The argument in favor of equal opportunities in medicine for minorities as a value and a goal has often been repeated in recent years in many places. But there is another justification that is often in the minds of those who advocate the policy of positive action by medical schools in behalf of minorities. As stated in the 1968 report of the Macy Foundation:

> The medical schools are accepting black students with marginal qualifications to right a social wrong [lack of equal opportunity] and hopefully to improve medical care for black society.[4]

The second reason then is to improve medical care for black society. There is no debate that, whether in inner cities or in rural areas, not only blacks as a whole but also the other underrepresented minorities have poorer access to health care than the majority and suffer greater disabilities in health. There *is* some debate, however, over the degree to which the education of more minority physicians will solve the health problems of minorities. It can at least be said that increasing the number of minority physicians may ameliorate, even if it will not solve, that social problem.[5] Even amelioration represents some social gain.

Whatever the validity of the argument that if more minorities are educated as physicians they will care for underserved minority communities and thus will reduce the embarrassingly low health statistics of minorities as compared with those of the majority in American society,[6] there remains the argument in support of social justice for minorities derived from the American belief in equality of opportunity for all. Since minority groups include a high proportion of individuals underprivileged in terms of access to equal educational opportunity—which leads in turn to their underrepresentation in medicine—this argument led at last to the conclusion within the white majority in the predominantly white medical schools that they should support a policy of positive action on behalf of minorities.

This policy was destined, however, to confront America with a second dilemma. The first, posed by Myrdal, was the discrepancy between the American equalitarian creed based on the proposition that all men are created free and equal, and the contradictory fact of legal slavery of

Black Americans. If slavery by law was abolished in the 1860s, unequal status survived by law in some states and by customary behavior patterns, in varying ways, in all states. As a consequence of the civil rights movement, judicial decisions and then legislation culminated in the 1950s and 1960s in forbidding in principle laws and practices that discriminated against anyone by reason of race. The principal beneficiaries of such actions have been Black Americans, American Indians, Mexican Americans, and Mainland Puerto Ricans, all of whom tend to share a darker skin coloring than the white majority. Under the new legal dispensation, racial discrimination was no longer allowed; prejudice against color as an influence on decisions affecting other human beings was to yield to color blindness.

By the mid-1960s, however, more and more observers concluded that past discriminatory actions against racial minorities, even if no longer enforced in decisions affecting them, still had consequences in the lives of many minority individuals that served to perpetuate their disadvantaged status and thus deterred them from achieving equality of opportunity. Something more is required, something positive—in Federalese, something "affirmative"—in the way of remedial, compensatory, or preferential opportunity to help minorities catch up with the majority so that they can participate ultimately on an even basis with the majority. In short, since racial minorities had been discriminated *against* for so long, and consequently had been confined to an underprivileged status, so—for a time at least—it would be necessary to discriminate *for* them in remedial ways to enable them to achieve equal status.

Beginning in 1968 medical schools developed a variety of positive or "affirmative" special programs intended to attract the interest of minority students, to admit them to medical school, to give them financial assistance, and to provide special cultural and psychological, as well as academic, support during their medical school years. These programs will be discussed in detail later, but first it must be noted that these positive efforts have come to be challenged as being discriminatory not only for minorities but also discriminatory against the white majority and therefore, it is claimed, unlawful. Because of the intensity of competition for the limited number of places in medical schools, it is understandable that special color-conscious policies regarding admission of minorities are the particular focus of attack as instances of "reverse discrimination." In 1969–70, 24,465 applicants filed 133,822 applications (an average of 5.5 by each applicant); of these applicants 43.1 percent were accepted. Despite the creation of a substantial number of new places, the competition increased. By 1973–74, 40,506 filed 328,275 applications (an average of 8.1), and only 35.4 percent received acceptances. The trauma surrounding such competition for admission could hardly fail to arouse intense scrutiny of admission criteria and procedures, especially by those denied admission to medical schools.

It so happens, however, that the first law case attracting national attention to this new dilemma about discrimination, namely discrimination *for* to overcome discrimination *against* being *reverse* discrimination, arose with regard to admission not to medical but to law school. For in this same period, law schools also experienced a sharp rise in applicants for a limited number of places. Concurrently they too had embarked on positive programs supportive of an increase in the number of students from minority groups, who have been seriously underrepresented in the legal profession as they have been in the medical profession.

It may well be that even as the first dilemma regarding race relations in the United States is associated with the name of Gunnar Myrdal, the second dilemma will be associated with that of Marco DeFunis. The latter was one of some 1,600 applicants to the University of Washington School of Law. The school's enrollment was limited to 150 in the first-year class, so the vast majority of applicants had to be denied admission. Marco DeFunis was one of them. This law school had developed positive programs to encourage the entry of minority students and, indeed, admitted some minority students who had grade point averages (GPAs) and/or Law School Admission Tests (LSATs) below those of DeFunis. Denied admission to the law school in 1970 and then in 1971, DeFunis protested through an attorney to university authorities but without avail. DeFunis then turned to the courts. Pending the conclusion of the trial, the superior court ordered that a place be held for DeFunis as a first-year student in the 1971–72 class. In September 1971 the trial judge rendered his opinion. Finding that some minorities had college grades and scores on aptitude tests below those of DeFunis, he held that the plaintiff had not been accorded equal protection of the law guaranteed by the Fourteenth Amendment and directed that the law school admit him to the first-year class. The judge commented:

> In 1954 the United States Supreme Court in *Brown* v. *the Board of Education* decided that public education must be equally available to all regardless of race.
>
> After that decision the Fourteenth Amendment could no longer be stretched to accommodate the needs of any race. Policies of dis-

crimination will inevitably lead to reprisals. In my opinion the only safe rule is to treat all races alike and I feel that is what is required under the equal protection clause.[7]

The University of Washington thereupon appealed from this judgment of the trial court to the Washington Supreme Court. DeFunis remained as a student under court order and was more than halfway through his second year of law school when the court rendered its judgment in March 1973. By a six-to-two vote the majority upheld the university and the preferential admissions policy for minorities. It rejected the trial court's insistence upon maintaining a color-blind view of all racial classifications. It found that a racial classification was constitutionally permissible if it could be shown as necessary to serve a "compelling state interest." Turning to the Fourteenth Amendment, the Washington Supreme Court quoted the U.S. Supreme Court as follows:

> The clear and central purpose of the Fourteenth Amendment was to eliminate all official state sources of invidious racial discrimination. . . . At the very least the Equal Protection Clause demands that racial classifications be subjected to "the most rigid scrutiny," and, if they are ever to be upheld, they must be shown to be necessary to the accomplishment of some permissible state objective independent of the racial discrimination which it was the object of the Fourteenth Amendment to eliminate.

The state court then continued:

> The burden is upon the law school to show that its consideration of race in admitting students is necessary to the accomplishment of a compelling state interest.

Noting that minorities were grossly underrepresented in the law schools and consequently in the legal profession, the court stated its belief that the state has an overriding interest in promoting integration in public education and in eliminating racial imbalance within public legal education. It also affirmed that the state has an overriding interest in providing all law students with a legal education that will adequately prepare them to deal with societal problems that will confront them on graduation. Hence it concluded that the educational interest of the state in producing a racially balanced student body at the law school is compelling.

The state court also said:

> It has been suggested that the minority admissions policy is not necessary, since the same objective could be accomplished by im-

proving the elementary and secondary education of minority students to a point where they could secure equal representation in law schools through direct competition with nonminority applicants on the basis of the same academic criteria. This would be highly desirable, but 18 years have passed since the decision in *Brown* v. *Board of Education,* and minority groups are still grossly underrepresented in law schools. If the law school is forbidden from taking affirmative action, this underrepresentation may be perpetuated indefinitely. No less restrictive means would serve the governmental interest here; we believe the minority admissions policy of the law school to be the only feasible "plan that promises realistically to work, and promises realistically to work *now.*"

The state court concluded that the defendants had shown the necessity of the racial classification for the accomplishment of an overriding state interest and had thus sustained the heavy burden imposed upon them, and that the denial of admission to DeFunis had not violated the Equal Protection Clause of the Fourteenth Amendment. Rejecting the argument that the admissions committee need base selection of students on purely mathematical ranking, it added:

Where the criteria for admissions are not arbitrary and capricious, we will not vitiate the judgment of the admissions committee unless a violation is shown. Considering the debatable nature of the criteria, we do not find the consideration of race in the admission of those minority applicants who indicate competence to successfully complete the law school program to be arbitrary and capricious. Law school admissions need not become a game of numbers; the process should remain sensitive and flexible, with room for informed judgment in interpreting mechanical indicators. The committee may consider the racial or ethnic background of an applicant when interpreting his standardized grades and test scores.

Thus in the opinions of the trial court and Supreme Court in Washington, two philosophies are juxtaposed. One is the simple and straightforward color-blind philosophy that rejects any form of racial classification *per se* and would thus reject any consideration of the still enduring consequences on the lives of both white and "colored" Americans of past discrimination, including even the legal acceptance until 1954 of a "separate but equal" constitutional interpretation for the status of blacks and the continuing separate status of American Indians for certain purposes. The other is the more complex color-conscious philosophy, accepting of the necessity of passing for a period of time through an evolutionary, acculturative, and remedial human process, if American society is to achieve equal protection of all Americans and true equality of opportunity for all its citizens.

As anticipated, DeFunis appealed from the opinion of the Washington Supreme Court to the U.S. Supreme Court, and Justice Douglas issued an order maintaining the status quo for DeFunis as a student while the case was appealed. The justices agreed to hear the case and invited briefs from the opposing attorneys, who brought to the attention of the court major constitutional and policy issues. The high level of nationwide concern for these issues is indicated by the fact that almost thirty briefs were submitted by more than fifty organizations or groups as friends of the court, representing both sides of the issues. The dilemma presented by the issues in this particular case caused sharp divisions even among organizations that had stood together in the civil rights cases in the 1950s and 1960s. For the U.S. Supreme Court, the case must also have posed difficult problems. On April 23, 1974, after having taken all the steps preliminary to reaching a decision, the Court decided not to decide the case by a five-to-four decision. Though the minority vigorously dissented and argued that the case should be decided to provide guidance in a troubled area of the law, the majority chose to regard the case as moot. Since DeFunis was already registered in his final quarter of law school, and since it was understood that he would remain a student of the law school for the duration of any term in which he had enrolled and hence would presumably be given an opportunity to complete the requirements for graduation, the Court concluded that he would receive his diploma regardless of any decision that it might make and therefore chose to dismiss the case as moot, thus ending any action on the merits.

So far as the University of Washington was concerned, the decision of the Washington Supreme Court was left standing, and the university has continued a positive policy on behalf of minorities in the law school as well as in its other schools and colleges—including the medical school.

There is no doubt, however, that the attention throughout all of higher education given to the controversy at issue in the DeFunis case strengthened the arguments of those opposed to special programs for minorities and aroused in those favoring them a concern for the possible imposition of legal restrictions, thus making them more cautious advocates. As the case moved through the courts, it quickly became known to medical schools and to the AAMC, which indeed submitted an *amicus curiae* brief to the U.S. Supreme Court. It noted that the interests of its member medical schools paralleled in nearly every respect those of the

Association of American Law Schools, and endorsed the positions and arguments in the latter's brief to the U.S. Supreme Court. Medical schools engaged in special programs for the admission of minority students began to receive threats of suit and actual suits from disappointed applicants. In the case of *Gray* v. *the Indiana University School of Medicine,* a superior court judge on August 15, 1974, upheld the medical school's "minority consideration program" as serving a compelling state interest in the education of minority students, creating a fair and equitable opportunity for economically and culturally deprived minority candidates to have their academic abilities fairly evaluated, and remedying a severe shortage of physicians. Hence the judge held that the applicant was not entitled to relief.[8]

Three months later, on November 25, 1974, the Medical School of the University of California at Davis fared differently in *Bakke* v. *Regents of the University of California.*[9] A superior court judge found its program to increase opportunities in medical education for disadvantaged citizens racially discriminating; and since the judge could not conclude that there was any compelling public purpose to be served in granting preference to minority students in admission when to do so denied white persons an equal opportunity, he held the program at Davis to be in violation of the Equal Protection Clause of the Fourteenth Amendment. In this case there was injected an additional issue that was not present in the fact situation in the DeFunis case, namely, the presence of the "quota" system, by which a given number of positions was reserved for disadvantaged students. Though this allegation was disputed by the medical school, the judge concluded that it had in fact established a quota for the so-called special program and was carrying it out in its admission practices. The regents of the university appealed to the California Supreme Court, whose six-to-one decision was handed down on September 16, 1976.[10]

Upholding the trial court's decision that the special admissions program was constitutionally invalid, the California Supreme Court returned the case to the trial court to determine whether the applicant would have been admitted to the 1973 or 1974 entering class if the special admissions program had not been in effect. The court held that the program as administered violates the constitutional rights of nonminority applicants because it affords preference on the basis of race to persons who, by the university's standards, are not as qualified for the study of medicine as nonminority students denied admission. The court held that since the special program involved classification by race, it was subject to strict scrutiny. Contrary to the opinion of the Washington Supreme Court in the DeFunis case, it concluded that the University of California had not established that its program, which discriminates against white applicants because of their race, was necessary to achieve the university's objectives of integrating the student body and, in this instance, of improving medical care for minorities. In reaching this conclusion, it emphasized that the university is not required to make admission decisions strictly on the basis of academic grades but may take the disadvantaged background into consideration, so long as admission standards are applied in a racially neutral fashion.

The court explained the policy considerations against a racially preferential admission policy in the following extract:

> The divisive effect of such preferences needs no explication and raises serious doubts whether the advantages obtained by the few preferred are worth the inevitable cost to racial harmony. The overemphasis upon race as a criterion will undoubtedly be counter-productive: rewards and penalties, achievements and failures, are likely to be considered in a racial context through the school years and beyond. Pragmatic problems are certain to arise in identifying groups which should be preferred or in specifying their numbers, and preferences once established will be difficult to alter or abolish; human nature suggests a preferred minority will be no more willing than others to relinquish an advantage once it is bestowed. Perhaps most important, the principle that the Constitution sanctions racial discrimination against a race—any race—is a dangerous concept fraught with potential for misuse in situations which involve far less laudable objectives than are manifest in the present case.

> We cannot agree with the proposition that deprivation based upon race is subject to a less demanding standard of review under the Fourteenth Amendment if the race discriminated against is the majority rather than a minority. We have found no case so holding, and we do not hesitate to reject the notion that racial discrimination may be more easily justified against one race than another, nor can we permit the validity of such discrimination to be determined by a mere census count of the races.

> Regardless of its historical origin, the equal protection clause by its literal terms applies to "any person," and its lofty purpose, to secure equality of treatment to all, is incompatible with the premise that some races may be afforded a higher degree of protection against unequal treatment than others.

We observe and emphasize in this connection that the University is not required to choose between a racially neutral admission standard applied strictly according to grade point averages and test scores, and a standard which accords preference to minorities because of their race.

In addition, the University may properly as it in fact does, consider other factors in evaluating an applicant, such as the personal interview, recommendations, character, and matters relating to the needs of the profession and society, such as an applicant's professional goals. In short, the standards for admission employed by the University are not constitutionally infirm except to the extent that they are utilized in a racially discriminatory manner. Disadvantaged applicants of all races must be eligible for sympathetic consideration, and no applicant may be rejected because of his race, in favor of another who is less well qualified, as measured by standards applied without regard to race. We reiterate, in view of the dissent's misinterpretation, that we do not compel the University to utilize only 'the highest objective academic credentials' as the criterion for admission.

In addition to flexible admission standards, the University might increase minority enrollment by instituting aggressive programs to identify, recruit, and provide remedial schooling for disadvantaged students of all races who are interested in pursuing a medical career and have an evident talent for doing so.

To uphold the University would call for the sacrifice of principle for the sake of dubious expediency and would represent a retreat in the struggle to assure that each man and woman shall be judged on the basis of individual merit alone, a struggle which has only lately achieved success in removing legal barriers to racial equality. The safest course, the one most consistent with the fundamental interests of all races and with the design of the Constitution is to hold, as we do, that the special admission program is unconstitutional because it violates the rights guaranteed to the majority by the equal protection clause of the Fourteenth Amendment of the United States Constitution.

In a dissenting opinion, Justice Tobriner pointed out that the medical school had voluntarily adopted the special admission program to overcome the segregation resulting from its past admission policies. The dissent observed that:

Two centuries of slavery and racial discrimination have left our nation an awful legacy, a largely separated society in which wealth, educational resources, employment opportunities—indeed all of society's benefits—remain largely the preserve of the white-Anglo majority. Until recently, most attempts to overcome the effects of this heritage of racial discrimination have proven unavailing. In the past decade, however, the implementation of numerous "affirmative action" programs, much like the program challenged in this case, have resulted in at least some degree of integration in many of our institutions.

To date, this court has always been at the forefront in protecting the rights of minorities to participate fully in integrated governmental institutions. It is anomalous that the Fourteenth Amendment that served as the basis for the requirement that elementary and secondary schools could be compelled to integrate, should now be turned around to forbid graduate schools from voluntarily seeking that very objective.

The dissent took issue with the majority's conclusion that the minority students accepted under the special admission program were "less qualified," under the medical school's own standards, than nonminority students rejected by the medical school. Pointing out that the record established that all the students accepted under the program were fully qualified for the study of medicine, the dissent maintained that

> . . . by adopting the special admission program, the medical school has indicated that in its judgment differences in academic credentials among qualified applicants are not the sole nor best criterion for judging how qualified an applicant is in terms of his potential to make a contribution to the medical profession or to satisfy needs of both the medical school and the medical profession that are not being met by other students.

Justice Tobriner took particular issue with the majority's suggestion that the goal of the special program for minorities could be achieved by ignoring racial and ethnic classification and by relying on a "disadvantage" standard. He stated:

> The majority initially suggest that the medical school could achieve its goals by utilizing such nonracial means as opening its special admission program to disadvantaged applicants of all races. This alternative—like most of the other nonracial classifications which have been suggested—bears the initial vice of disingenuousness. Because the principal objective of the medical school is to achieve a *racially* and *ethnically* integrated, rather than an economically diverse, student body, any nonracial classification will achieve the

medical school's objective only to the extent that such nonracial classification in fact correlates with minority race and ethnic background. Thus, the process of selecting a racially neutral criterion to promote integration cannot honestly be described as a "nonracial" decision. Yet the majority commands just such a manipulation of labels, so that the perfectly proper purposes of the program must be concealed by subterfuge. I do not concur in this retreat into obfuscating terminology.

Moreover, although the majority speculate that the broadening of the special admission program to disadvantaged applicants of all races will result in approximately the same amount of integration as the present program, that conclusion appears untenable on its face. Because all disadvantaged students need financial aid, the total number of such students a medical school can afford to admit is limited. As a consequence, inclusion of all disadvantaged students in the special admission program would inevitably decrease the number of minority students admitted under the program and thus curtail the achievement of all integration-related objectives.

In his dissenting opinion Justice Tobriner also disposed of another alternative suggested by the majority:

The majority's alternative suggestion that the integration of medical schools can be accomplished by increasing the size and number of medical schools is similarly unrealistic. The cost of medical educational facilities is enormous; absolutely nothing suggests that the necessary financial commitment for increased facilities will be forthcoming in the foreseeable future. It is a cruel hoax to deny minorities participation in the medical profession on the basis of such clearly fanciful speculation.

While recognizing that racial classifications had frequently been used to discriminate against disfavored minority groups, Justice Tobriner observed that:

The racial classifications at issue in this case are worlds apart from the invidious racial classifications deemed constitutionally suspect in prior cases. The racial classifications embodied in the special admission program are not intended to, nor do they in fact, exclude any particular racial group from participation in the medical school; on the contrary, the program is aimed at assuring that qualified applicants of all racial groups are actually represented in the institution.

The dissent finally explained that:

Numerous decisions recognize that as a practical matter racial classifications frequently must be employed if the effects of past discrimination and exclusion are to be overcome and if integration of currently segregated institutions is to be achieved; these cases establish that the Constitution does not forbid such use of remedial racial classifications. By failing to distinguish between *invidious racial classifications* and remedial or *"benign" racial classifications,* the majority utilize the wrong constitutional standard in evaluating the validity of the Davis special admission program. This fundamental error inevitably infects and invalidates the majority's ultimate constitutional conclusion.

The University of California has appealed the decision to the U.S. Supreme Court.

In another challenge of the admissions process by a medical school applicant, the New York Court of Appeals in the case of *Alevy* v. *Downstate Medical Center of the State of New York* [11] rendered an opinion on April 8, 1976, essentially contrary to that of the California court. Maintaining that in proper circumstances reverse discrimination is constitutional, the court held that it must be shown that a substantial state interest underlies the preferential treatment policy and that no less objectionable alternative will serve the same purposes. Although the school practiced reverse discrimination as regards admission of minority applicants, the court found, it was not necessary to inquire whether there were less objectionable alternatives, since even if the entire minority program were eliminated, the petitioner would still not have been entitled to a position in the 1974–75 class. Thus, while dismissing the appeal on the grounds that the petitioner's relative standing with respect to other nonminority applicants was such that he could not assert a claim of harm from the admission granted to minorities, the court engaged in an interesting dictum:

The Fourteenth Amendment was adopted to guarantee equality for blacks, and by logical extension has come to include all minority groups. Thus, strict scrutiny is clearly warranted in order that its mandate be carried forth. Additionally, the amendment has been interpreted as permitting, if in fact not requiring, the correction of historical invidious discriminations. It would indeed be ironic, and of course, would cut against the very grain of the amendment, were the Equal Protection Clause used to strike down measures designed to achieve real equality for persons whom it was intended to aid. We reject, therefore, the strict scrutiny test for benign discrimination as, in our view, such an application would be contrary to the salutary purposes for which the Fourteenth Amendment was intended.

Thus, the Washington Supreme Court subjected the law school admissions program for minorities to "strict scrutiny" and concluded that it met the more difficult test of fulfilling a "compelling" or "overriding" state interest. The California Supreme Court also subjected the medical school special admissions program to "strict scrutiny" but concluded that it was not necessary to meet a compelling state interest. The New York Court of Appeals believed it might be sufficient to meet a less stringent test, the middle ground of a "substantial" state interest to make acceptable the use of racial classifications for benign purposes. It stated:

> We are of the view that in deciding an issue of whether reverse discrimination is present, the courts should make proper inquiry to determine whether the preferential treatment satisfies a substantial State interest. In determining whether a substantial State interest underlies a preferential treatment policy, courts should inquire whether the policy has a substantial basis in actuality, and is not merely conjectural. At a minimum, the State-sponsored scheme must further some legitimate, articulated governmental purpose. However, the interest need not be urgent, paramount or compelling. Then, to satisfy the substantial interest requirement, it need be found that, on balance, the gain to be derived from the preferential policy outweighs its possible detrimental effects. . . .

> In sum, in proper circumstances, reverse discrimination is constitutional. However, to be so, it must be shown that a substantial interest underlies the policy and practice, and, further, that no nonracial, or less objectionable racial, classifications will serve the same purpose. . . .

> On the other hand, however, our recognition that benign discrimination is permissible should not be taken as tacit approval of such practices. We reiterate that preferential policies, laudable in origin and goal, may be laden with detrimental side effects which make their use undesirable. If such practices really work, the period and extent of their use should be temporary and limited for as goals are achieved, their utilization should be diminished. Conversely, if no improvement is noted, consideration should be given to the discontinuation of the practice.

Advocates of positive programs for minorities, of course, regard them as temporary expedients to overcome the consequences of past discrimination and of definitely disadvantaged status in American society, expedients the success of which would eliminate the reasons for their continued existence. It is not known whether the Downstate Medical School's admissions program would have met this court's test of fulfilling a substantial state interest in a manner that could not be served by the use of a nonracial or less objectionable racial classification, since the judges did not find it necessary to reach a conclusion on this matter in the particular case in question.

Similar challenges to special consideration of minority applicants may well appear again in the courts, and someday the U.S. Supreme Court may provide the most authoritative legal decisions on the matter. In any case, there is authority to support the legality of progressing from insistence upon the absolute color-blind test to some form of race-conscious considerations, where the purpose of discrimination may be ruled benign and a form of "reverse discrimination" may be interpreted as constitutionally acceptable. Perhaps some details of procedure may be restricted as beyond the law, but it remains possible also that what the advocates of positive remedial programs for minorities deem wise social policy responsive to the laws of human behavior may also be acceptable to the law of the land. Or it may even be that the justices of the U.S. Supreme Court will act so as to reveal their concurrence with the opinion of Archibald Cox that:

> The time for a rigid constitutional rule has not yet come. It is better to permit the State educational authorities to form their several individual judgments concerning the balance of educational and social advantage than to deny them freedom to attempt conscious remedies for past racial discrimination by the dominant whites.[12]

In the interim it is obviously desirable for medical schools to watch this legal front with the help of lawyers. No final answer is yet available to the question as to whether medical schools may constitutionally take race or minority origin as an element in selecting students for admission, but there are some grounds to conclude that the courts

1. will not require admissions committees to rely solely on "objective criteria" in making selection decisions;

2. will expect admission policies to be clearly defined and available to applicants;

3. will require special admissions programs to be justified at least as necessary to fulfill a substantial state interest;

4. will expect admissions committees to adhere strictly to their published criteria and procedures;

5. will, to their utmost, avoid having to substitute judicial opinion for that of educational authorities;

6. will avoid granting equitable relief to plaintiffs where, at least, the defendant institution has shown that such plaintiffs would not have been admitted even without the allegedly offensive aspect of the program.

Special admission programs for minorities and the problem of reverse discrimination are troubled and troublesome matters both within and without medical schools. For further clarification of the issues included in determining the rightness or wrongness of positive programs for minorities as to policy and to law, one can do no better than to read carefully the dispassionate analysis of a lawyer who is also vice-president of Indiana University at Bloomington, Robert M. O'Neil, in his *Discriminating Against Discrimination, Preferential Admissions and the DeFunis Case.*[13]

Whether one is for or against preferential admissions, anyone interested in this subject would find this succinct treatment in layman's language informative. The following quick summary is intended as an invitation to, and not as a substitute for, reading O'Neil's own words.

He begins with a summary of the facts and issues in the DeFunis case and of the opinions rendered by the Washington courts and then reviews the actions of the U.S. Supreme Court that culminated in its decision not to decide the case. Turning to preferential admissions as they appear in higher education, he notes that admissions officers, at least in selective institutions, have long realized that intelligent and responsible choices among applicants cannot be made solely on the basis of quantitative and impersonal factors. Except in those instances where an open-door policy mandates acceptance of every student who applies with a diploma or a degree, the process is highly complex; for, in addition to the almost universally prerequisite high school or undergraduate grades and scores on standardized tests, numerous other elements may be—and are—considered. Among them are letters of recommendation from former teachers, counselors, family friends, clergymen, and others; appraisal by a principal, dean, or other academic administrator; personal interviews; the applicant's own statement of his affiliations, interests, or goals; and the record of his extracurricular achievements and community service. What are usually regarded as easy cases, applications of students with very superior or inferior academic records, may be resolved essentially on the basis of mathematical factors, but other factors may be more heavily considered for applicants in the middle range. Sometimes a nonacademic factor, an evidence of a special interest or skill desired in the student mix, may cause a departure from strict numerical ranking and constitute a clear form of preferential admission of candidates. Athletic skill may be one of the more notorious reasons for preferential admissions, but there are less debated ones. Preference may be granted on occasion to children of alumni, faculty, friends of the institution, legislators and other public officials, or to veterans. Adjustment of admissions criteria has been thought warranted for the physically handicapped (blind, deaf, disabled); for recent arrivals from abroad whose education has been in a foreign land and foreign tongue; even for reasons of sex until recently; and for geographical considerations, either to encourage diversity of regional origin or, in the opposite direction, to restrict the number of out-of-state residents. The novelty of the 1960s, then, was not the departure from strict numerical ranking of applicants but, rather, the addition of race to other factors on which preference had long been based.

O'Neil then briefly surveys the place of minority students in higher education. He notes their small percentage when national data first began to be collected in 1967 and their general increase up to 1972, followed by a fall in 1973 and 1974. He describes the uneven distribution of minorities with between one-third and two-fifths of all blacks in traditionally black colleges. The remainder, along with other minorities, are disproportionately concentrated in major urban commuter campuses and are found largely in the underclass years with high attrition rates that reduce the numbers advancing to graduation and postgraduate years. Recently special programs have increased the numbers entering postbaccalaureate fields of study. O'Neil sketches in particular recent developments with regard to minority students in legal education, which in many ways parallel developments in medical education.

Against this background O'Neil then explores some of the legal problems and issues that may be raised by consideration of race in the admissions policy, noting in particular that the U.S. Supreme Court has stopped short of holding racial distinctions *per se* invalid, possibly allowing them in a case where a compelling state interest can be shown to be served by their use. O'Neil then presents, as he sees it, the case for preferential admissions: the effects of minority underrepresentation, the effects of traditional entrance criteria, the need to compensate for the effects of past discrimination, and the necessity that the university as a microcosm represent the larger society and prepare its students for responsible and meaningful citizenship. Exploring possible nonracial alternatives, he finds that—sound though they may be for other reasons —they fail to meet the needs or goals for which preferential policies were designed.

O'Neil then describes the case against preferential admissions. The most persuasive argument may well be the most obvious: any consideration of race, whether to help or to harm minority groups, officially sanctions a distinction that we have been trying for decades to minimize. Racial classifications are inherently divisive and acquire added importance from governmental recognition. Racial distinctions themselves are immutable and indelible without the government's calling attention to them. The power to classify on the basis of race, no matter how allegedly "benign" the goal, is admittedly dangerous. It is also feared that racial prejudice rejects or abandons the historic American commitment to merit and ability in selecting students. In the discussion of "merit" and "qualification," they are often assumed to be synonymous with numerical ranking. A closely related fear is that preference soon leads to quotas, which are abhorrent to responsible educators. Despite the insistence that many preferential programs work toward "goals" and not "quotas," many find the distinction specious when it is made. There have been instances of admission procedures using quotas, but other schools have had goals that are different from quotas. There are also effects of preferential admissions on nonminority groups as well upon minorities themselves, such as the stigma that may be attached to preferential treatment and the exposure to socially difficult situations on a white-Anglo campus. (I shall return to this problem at some length.)

For O'Neil the argument for preferential admission still prevails, and he closes with a brief discussion of the policy implications of preferential admissions under the headings of five questions:

1. Who may or should be preferred under such a policy?
2. In what form should the preference be extended?
3. How much preference is appropriate?
4. How long should preferential policies last?
5. What are the practical responsibilities of a college or university that adopts preferential policies?

Before leaving this matter of preferential treatment, however, it should be added that the underlying philosophical controversy over discrimination and reverse discrimination, while it surfaced as a legal issue in the context of admissions, also pervades discussions of many other aspects of special programs for minorities, stalking the corridors of medical schools well after the students have been admitted to their precincts.[14]

NOTES

1. Edward W. Brice, "The Conservation of Human Resources," 443 (see note 5, Chapter 2).

2. Hutchins *et al.*, "Minorities, Manpower, and Medicine," 809–821 (see note 3, Chapter 2).

3. AAMC, *Task Force Report 1970* (see note 11, Chapter 2).

4. Josiah Macy, Jr. Foundation, *Annual Report for the Year 1968*, p. 16 (see note 8, Chapter 2).

5. James L. Curtis, *Blacks, Medical Schools, and Society* (Ann Arbor: University of Michigan Press, 1971): pp. 147–163.

6. *Minority Health Chart Book,* American Public Health Association Report for 102nd Annual Meeting, pp. 32–41, 48–52, 60–73 (see note 2, Chapter 3).

7. This and subsequent references to the DeFunis case are from Ann Fagan Ginger, ed., *DeFunis Versus Odegaard and the University of Washington, The University Admissions Case* (Dobbs Ferry, New York: Oceana Publications, Inc., 1974): I: 116, 155–6, 160, 165; III: 1349–1393. Because of the widespread interest in the issues raised in this case and their extensive analysis in the briefs and opinions, virtually the entire record of this litigation including the many briefs submitted by friends of the court has been published in these three volumes.

8. *Gray* v. *The Indiana University School of Medicine* (Marion County Superior Court, August 15, 1974).

9. *Bakke* v. *Regents of the University of California* No. 31,287 (Yolo County Superior Court, November 25, 1974).

10. *Bakke* v. *Board of Regents, University of California*, 132 Cal. Rptr. 680, 553 P. 2d 1152 (September 16, 1976). The paragraphs from the majority opinion quoted in the text are, in order, from the following pages in 553 P. 2d: 1171, 1163, 1165, 1166, 1171. The paragraphs from the dissenting opinion quoted in the text are, in order, from the following pages in 553 P. 2d: 1191, 1173, 1190, 1175, 1173.

11. *Alevy* v. *Downstate Medical Center of the State of New York,* 384 New York Supplement, 2d Series, 82, 89, 90, 91 (Court of Appeals, 1976).

12. Archibald Cox, *The Role of the Supreme Court in American Government* (New York: Oxford University Press, 1976): p. 68.

13. Robert M. O'Neil, *Discriminating Against Discrimination, Preferential Admissions and the DeFunis Case* (Bloomington: Indiana University Press, 1975).

14. An interesting treatment of the legal issues presented in this chapter is contained in a recent publication, *Minority Group Participation in Graduate Education* (Washington, D.C.: Report No. 5 of the National Board on Graduate Education, June 1976): pp. 129–140.

Chapter 5
The Matter of Money

Money being the root of so much, a few words about it are in order. The focus of this report is on medical schools and what they can and should do to improve the situation of minorities in medicine. In all fairness, it must be said that the task is not one for medical schools alone. It will be remembered that the AAMC Task Force included a chart describing the educational flow, the student's movement through successive stages to the M.D. degree. It also depicted reasons for a student's possible exit from the flow at successive stages and designated so-called action elements, which could help to keep the student within the flow. These agents constitute a long list: the student himself, whose work, study, and self-motivation are fundamental ingredients; student groups; educational institutions of many kinds other than medical schools (as well as medical schools); minority community groups; the practicing medical profession; other private organizations and industry; medical and health associations, both regional and national; federal, state, and local governments; financial institutions; and foundations.[1] The success of this endeavor to increase minorities in medicine assuredly does turn on help from many sources for many things. The medical schools are far from being the only parties involved.

Medical schools, however, must play a key role in developing and servicing any program for minorities in medicine: they must be the pivot upon which the enterprise turns. Without their substantial commitment, involvement, and action, the fragments contributed by other agencies cannot fall into a coherent pattern and produce a flow of physicians. What the medical schools do and how well they do it, therefore, is of fundamental importance to the task of organizing opportunities for minorities in medicine and of achieving the result of having more minority physicians.

Medical education, it need hardly be said, is expensive for the student himself, in the sense of the fees paid medical schools as well as the costs of subsistence during four years of undergraduate preparation. The matter of financial aid is especially vital for minority students, since they typically come from backgrounds of poverty or relatively low socioeconomic status, and their needs on the average exceed those of the majority as a group. That there is a growing problem in providing financial assistance to needy nonminority as well as minority students is well known. Scholarships and loans in varying combinations from federal and state governments, corporations, and foundations, as well as personal gifts and university-endowed financial aid funds, have all helped keep needy students in school, as has money earned by students themselves or contributed by their families.

In the early 1960s, when fewer minority students were enrolled in medical schools, a needy minority student who had reached the point of admission to a medical school generally had a good chance of being relieved of the payment of fees and could be assured while a student of at least a subsistence level of existence from various sources available to the medical school. The disparity in economic circumstances between minority and nonminority students often dictated that minority students could qualify for funds available on a need basis ahead of most majority students.

Since 1973, however, several factors have made it more difficult to assure the availability of financial aid to minority as well as majority students in medicine and in higher education in general. They include the uncertainty as to government aid programs; economic depression influencing the availability of private funds, whether from corporations, foundations, medical school scholarship endowment funds, or individual contributions; rising prices increasing the dollar needs of students; and the greater number of minority students enrolled in medical schools. Medical schools are finding that they can offer fewer assurances as to support levels or that they have had to reduce the number of students to whom they can offer the probability of financial assistance at a subsistence level. It seems highly probable that this financial problem contributed to the subsidence in minority first-year enrollment from 1974–75 to 1975–76.

If this matter is not further discussed here, it is not because it is unimportant. It is, rather, because it is a discrete problem capable of analysis by itself and because there are agencies that are already much concerned with it, organized to deal with it more effectively, and positioned to act as continually informed advocates before possible funding agencies. One thinks particularly of the AAMC and the National Medical Fellowships, Incorporated.

To reiterate, the relatively brief treatment here of the needs of minority students for financial assistance is no measure of the central importance of such enlarged financial support to their ability to continue on the pathway to medical education. It is attributable to the recognition that others are better able to collect and analyze the appropriate data and to present the case for such assistance to all funding sources, public and private.

The recipient of medical education, the student, has financial problems in surviving as a medical student, the student from minority background assuredly so. But the provider of this education, the medical school, has its financial problems in surviving as a viable institution capable of rendering the educational service; these financial problems are intensified when a school incurs the increased costs associated with the additional services necessitated by its incorporation of increasing numbers of minority students into its student body. In recent years medical schools, public and private, have had increasing difficulty in maintaining—much less enlarging—the scope of their services. At such times, at the first suggestion of an action that would cost money or more money, the proposer is likely to be greeted with charges of impracticality or irresponsibility. This reaction is likely to be heightened if the proposer does not turn immediately to the matter of money and tell where the funds to cover the costs will come from or offer an easy solution.

This reaction is understandable as a first thought, but it should not be allowed to stop one's thinking about what ought to be done and how one ought to do it. Only at the end of such a process can a sound case be built for what ought to be done. If such a process is undertaken, despite the probability that the proposed program will entail additional costs, the chances are improved that those associated with the diverse sources of funds may be persuaded to give their support. It is admitted that this report is written in humility but also in the hope that it may be sufficiently persuasive to attract favorable attention within medical schools and within the funding sources to the continued and improved programs that are still required to facilitate the movement of more minority students into medicine.

NOTES

1. Bernard W. Nelson, Richard A. Bird, and Gilbert M. Rodgers, "Educational Pathway Analysis for the Study of Minority Representation in Medical School," *Journal of Medical Education* 46 (September 1971): 745–748.

Chapter 6
Opening Medical Schools to Minorities—
A Major Challenge

Before turning to a consideration of specific programs to encourage the movement of more students of minority origin through medical schools, it is only fair to note that the adoption of such programs constituted a major challenge to medical schools. It required changes by medical faculties in their customary assumptions, practices, and attitudes, which had been responses to existing circumstances.

Medical schools stood in a particular relationship to the academic structure at lower levels in the educational sequence. Because of extreme competition for entrance, medical faculties had become accustomed to students who were highly proficient in particular academic skills in which they had been extensively drilled prior to admission. These same students were drawn heavily from white middle-class families. Both circumstances affected faculty perceptions of their teaching responsibilities. Medical faculty members themselves being very predominantly white, they reflected, consciously or unconsciously, certain attitudes toward, and expectations of, students. Their own educational background tended to be such as not to help them become more aware of the effects of racism upon themselves and upon others. Not by reason of intent but as the consequence of a combination of circumstances, medical faculties in particular were not well prepared to undertake the adjustments required to introduce more minority persons to medicine. Even so, substantial change did occur through the initiative of medical schools. I turn now to the reasons why this development was a major challenge for medical schools.

Given the pressures upon universities in the past generation, it is easy for a faculty to become engrossed in its internal affairs, yet it should be mindful of its place within the larger structure of higher education. It needs to consider the circumstances affecting student applicants and the process through which they have passed in the attempt to become qualified to enter a higher level of instruction. It should also be aware of the dynamism of education and of the changing circumstances that affect the preparation and selection of its students.

It is sobering to recall, by way of example, that when law and medicine were added in the third quarter of the nineteenth century to the already established program in arts at the University of Michigan, secondary school graduates were all admissible to the law school, medical school, and arts college. The law students, however, received their LL.B. after only two years of attendance (each academic year being of only six months' duration); the medical students received their M.D. after three years (their academic year being nine months long); but the arts students faced four years of instruction (in a nine-month academic year) before they received an A.B. or B.S. degree.

One of the reforms supported by Flexner in 1910 was to move the medical curriculum to an upper level where students would be admitted only after two years of instruction in college, primarily in science. It may be commonplace now, with only occasional exceptions, that medical students are accepted only after completion of a four-year undergraduate degree and that expectations concerning the nature of academic preparation have stabilized on a heavy emphasis on course work in biology, physics, and chemistry.

Medical schools, like other instructional units, are enmeshed in a complex web of relationships with other elements in the structure of education. Separately organized teaching corps operate at successive levels: schools (education), colleges (higher education), and a plethora of graduate and advanced professional schools (sometimes called higher higher education). The more advanced its place within the sequence, the more a teaching corps tends to divide into separate specialized groups. Moving upward through this maze, students pursue courses of instruction that must be acceptable for certification of completion of the required curriculum at each level and that must also serve as suitable preparation for admission to a higher unit. A curriculum reasonably satisfactory to teachers in both the earlier and later units in the sequence is often established only after long and painful negotiations. Once a compromise has been reached, the two teaching corps usually relax to go about their own internal business; but various forces continue to play upon each level, leading to changed circumstances, practices, and expectations that gradually upset the equilibrium earlier established. At some point the dissatisfaction, caused by conflicting demands and poor articulation, finally induces reconsideration of the relationships; and a new episode of discussion and negotiation may begin, in the hope of leading to an updated, reasonably satisfactory compromise and to a better understanding by teachers at both levels of the type of counsel and instruction to be given to the student.

There is certainly a strong tendency for each separately organized faculty to prefer to concentrate its attention upon its own internal program rather than upon its external relations and the articulation of its efforts with those below or above in the sequence followed by students. By virtue of their special responsibilities, administrative officers such as principals, superintendents, and deans are more likely to encounter early the issues associated with conflicting objectives and poor articulation. However, they often find that it is not easy to elicit teacher or faculty involvement in the discussion process that is necessary to find remedies for the situation and to ease the transition between levels for the student.

If a faculty is a relative newcomer, endeavoring to expand instruction in a new or less established discipline or to alter the socially perceived role of its discipline or profession toward a more advanced or prestigious one, it is likely to be concerned with winning recruits in the form of more students. It will then be more disposed to engage in proselytizing activities outside its own walls addressed to teachers and students lower in the sequence. If, on the other hand, a faculty finds itself gatekeeper to a highly prestigious field with more than enough applicants appearing outside its walls seeking admission to a limited number of places, there will be less inducement to spend time outside its own environment in recruiting interest in its field. It will not even have to spend much time worrying about the provision of adequate preparation for its students or engaging in discussions with those who provide it. For with a substantial excess of applicants, it has only to announce the criteria of preparation that will guide it in granting admission. The numerous students at the lower level, seeing themselves as future applicants to the higher unit, will then exert pressure on the lower school to provide instruction in the courses demanded as preparation for admission.

In the past two decades medical schools have increasingly found applicants knocking at their gates and presenting records of qualitative fulfillment of prescribed requirements—in such numbers as to make it easy to fill entering classes with students capable of advancing in the curriculum with a very high degree of acceptability to the faculty. For example, the number of medical students who failed to graduate with the M.D. degree four years after matriculation decreased steadily from 13.7 percent in 1961 to 5.3 percent in 1967.[1] Of course some of these graduated later, and not all who withdrew did so for reasons of academic deficiency. From 1965–66 to 1974–75 all withdrawals from the medical school enrollment declined, for the most part steadily, from 3.19 percent to 1.83 percent; withdrawals for academic reasons shrank from 1.65 percent to 0.45 percent, while throughout these years withdrawals to pursue advanced study in other fields ran close to 0.33 percent.[2] Under these circumstances there has been little pressure to induce medical faculties to concern themselves directly with school or college faculties about the preparatory process or with promotional activities intended to encourage interest in medicine by prospective students. Far from facing a problem of recruiting applicants, medical schools have faced with increasing pressure for two decades the problem of rejecting even those who are qualified.

The impact on medical schools of the efforts since 1968 to introduce more minorities into the student mix cannot be understood without a clear perception of the extreme wrenching that this effort caused in the pattern of student admission, which had come to be viewed as customary by medical school faculties. Over the past twenty years no one has studied more systematically and consistently the selection system for medical students and their characteristics than Dr. Daniel H. Funkenstein of the Harvard Medical School. He has collected large amounts of data on Harvard Medical School classes since 1957; in the late 1960s he expanded his base to include data on students at Vanderbilt and Colorado;[3] and in the 1970s he has amassed data on students in a sample of twelve medical schools, the results of which are yet to be published. While his published material may be heavily based on studies of Harvard medical students, his findings may be taken as having a rough validity for students in most other medical schools; for Harvard reflects the kind of "scientific model" to which most medical faculties had come to adhere by the late 1960s.

In an unpublished paper Funkenstein has described five distinct eras through which medicine has passed since the Flexner report in 1910, eras during which the social responsibility, society's expectation of physicians, the assignment of priorities in medicine, and the funding of careers changed. These changes had profound effects on the career choices of graduating physicians and were caused largely because of societal factors over which medical schools or the profession had little control. The earlier eras were the General Practice Era, 1910–40; the Specialty Era, 1941–58; and the Scientific Era, 1959–68.[4]

To understand not only the medical school setting into which minority student recruitment and admission activities entered in a burst of enthusiasm in 1968, but also the more recent reaction in medical schools critical of special efforts on behalf of minorities, it is essential that one have clearly in mind the situation that developed in medical schools in the recent past. During this period the Scientific Era from 1959 to 1968 was followed by the brief but enthusiastic Community Era, 1969–71, which included a surge of interest in increasing the number of minority and women students, only to give way to what Funkenstein calls the Doldrums, 1971–present. He describes this era as, among other things, a return to a situation where the pool of applicants includes even more highly qualified persons in bioscience; "if current admission policies continue," he writes, "within a few years almost all students will be bioscientific." [5]

Only if one understands the general characteristics of medical schools as they had developed by 1968 can one understand the enormity of the challenge for change presented by the proposal to recruit and admit minority students. The need for such understanding warrants a lengthy quotation in which Funkenstein describes the basic characteristics of medical schools during the Scientific Era (1959–68), along with suggestions as to what he believes should have occurred:

The Socio-Economic Backgrounds of Medical Students

During the years 1959–1968, the socio-economic background of medical students did not change from what it had been in the past. The great majority were white males. In 1968–69, 91.2% of medical students were men and 8.8% were women; only 4.4% were minority group students. These figures are comparable to those for 1958–59.

The majority students were from upper-middle class families with incomes in excess of $10,000. Many of their fathers were professionals, the majority of whom had attended college. Few children of blue collar workers, farmers, or from lower class families were enrolled in medical school.

Values

Given such a population, the dominant values were a future orientation that allowed immediate pleasures to be deferred in lieu of an almost certain reward later; a belief in the work ethic, and a view that the individual is paramount, having control over his own destiny with outside forces playing little part in success or failure. Competition was valued because in this way merit would be rewarded—the survival of the fittest. There was the feeling that the individual could accomplish anything if he just worked hard enough; failure was the fault of the individual, not society.

The Development of Medical Schools into Scientific Institutions
During these years, the nation's medical schools became predominantly scientific institutions. After Sputnik was launched in 1958, billions of dollars were poured into scientific research. Science education was upgraded in secondary schools, colleges, graduate schools and medical schools to such an extent that the teaching of science in the first year of medical school was indistinct from that taught in colleges and universities.

As the Scientific Era began, it affected those medical schools best prepared to embrace the new opportunities. However, as these school[s] educated more scientists than they could appoint to their own faculties, their graduates secured faculty appointments at other medical schools. It was not long before superbly trained scientists made up, not only the preclinical faculty, but the clinical faculty as well, at all medical schools.

Values
The values of the scientific faculty were intellectual rigor, scientific research, and scholarly achievement. One of the byproducts of these values was intense competition for grants, for student-scientists, and even a demand for high grades on the National Boards. Board scores were sent to each school listing their relative standing to other schools. If a particular school slipped in its standing, faculty expressed great concern and action was usually taken to reverse this. For example, one school which began to fall in its ranking, required the National Board scores as an integral part of the final grade in each basic science course, believing that the students would try harder, and thus raise the image of the school. The embracing of this competitive ethic was well stated by Brooks in his 1971 C.P. Snow lecture titled, "Can Science Survive the Modern Age?"

'The achievement of scientific excellence is highly dependent on the protestant ethic of work and individual achievement. Although the scientific community is one of the most open of all social systems in terms of all criteria other than its own internal standards of performance, its insistence on individual excellence and on rigorous interpersonal valuations runs strongly counter to contemporary egalitarian trends and rejection of all competition and comparisons between people, especially among youth. In the current jargon science is an inherently "elitist" activity, and its success as a social institution is highly dependent upon a rigorous selection and ranking of its practitioners by their colleagues and seniors. As science has become professionalized in the last generation, its competitiveness has, if anything, increased. Some very able and talented people seem to be rejecting the "rat race" . . . the advance of science does depend on a process of natural selection of ideas and people not unlike biological evolution, and without this selective pressure, truth cannot avoid being swamped by error in the long run. Just as biological evolution runs against the average trend of the second law of thermodynamics, so does science run strongly against the social second law of the last common denominator.'

Differences Among Medical Schools

All medical schools were not alike. In 1957, Funkenstein described a continuum of medical schools, at one end of which were schools termed "ideistic," at the other end, those termed extremely "pragmatic." In the former were schools where students and faculty were concerned with abstract ideas and the search for truth, which were then reapplied to concrete problems. In the latter were schools where the students and faculty were concerned with the direct solution of concrete problems. The former schools produced academicians and physicians in the subspecialties; the latter schools graduated physicians in general or specialty practice with a large component of primary care in their practices.

By 1969, as the scientific revolution spread to all schools, all faculties became ideistic in their values, primarily interested in the abstract concepts related to disease processes and in research. They were more challenged by the tough, intellectually difficult diagnostic problems on the wards than by the routine day-to-day care of patients in the outpatient department, which they viewed as intellectually unstimulating.

However, many of the students were still pragmatically oriented, contrary to the wishes of their faculties who preferred the idealistically oriented, scientific student. The pool of applicants to medical school did not contain sufficient students of the preferred type, so many schools were forced to accept students who were oriented pragmatically toward people and service and planned a large element of primary care in their practices. These students have been described by me as student-practitioners, in contrast to the scientifically oriented students who were classified as student-scientists. A third type was the student-psychiatrist. Student-practitioners had lower MCAT scores; lower college GPA's; came from less well educated families; had marked interpersonal skills; and were devoted to service and working with people. Often they had participated widely in extracurricular activities. *Student-scientists* usually came from professional families; had very high MCAT's, especially in the quantitative and science subtests; had high college GPA's; had attended outstanding secondary schools; had majored in biology or chemistry; done summer research; and were devoted to the intellectual life. They had minimal participation in extracurricular activities, and were not as skilled in interpersonal relationships.

Because the great majority of student-scientists went to graduate school in the physical sciences, chemistry, or biology, there were insufficient student-scientists in the applicant pool to medical school. This was the only constraint that prevented all medical schools from selecting only student-scientists, thus making their student bodies as well as their faculties ideistic in their value orientation.

Academic Standards
During the 1960's, the changed characteristics and values of faculties, and the marked improvement of the premedical science education of students caused a dramatic increase in academic standards of medical schools.

Educational Aims—Careers
As the Scientific Era developed, the career plans of medical students changed from private, specialty practice with a large component of primary care, to academic medicine or a subspecialty with little or no primary care in their practices. This was due to the increasing opportunities in academic medicine and the presence in the medical school of faculties composed primarily of scientists who acted as role models. It is not surprising that these faculties sought to reproduce themselves. They wanted to graduate physicians who were primarily scientists, who would do research with some patient care, or would be in a bioscientifically oriented clinical subspecialty with a medical school affiliation. Sanazaro found that in a national sample of interns during 1958–59, 27% planned careers in academic medicine; in 1964–65, this percentage had risen to 38%. Certainly by 1968, this figure was even higher.

The Curriculum
During the development of the Scientific Era, the curriculum changed in the direction of higher academic standards, and increasing the amount of material in basic science, which was taught at a more quantitative level, and which was more and more irrelevant to the practice of medicine. No changes were made to accomodate [sic] the greater diversity in the preparation of entering students. This diversity was due to differences in the preparation of

student scientists, student-practitioners, and student-psychiatrists. The curriculum was geared to the better scientifically prepared students.

Colleges, unlike medical schools who did not give credit for medical school courses studied in college, gave credit for college level courses studied in high school and developed several levels of beginning courses in biology, chemistry, mathematics, and physics, entrance to which depended upon the students' previous education. Our studies of the relationship between preparation and grades in medical school showed that in the 1950's grades in college science courses correlated with grades in medical school; in the 1960's, this correlation fell, but a high correlation was obtained between the level of a student's preparation and his medical school grades. For example, grades in the genetics courses at Harvard Medical School correlated .86 with having a genetics course in college.

Another aspect of the diversity of students was not accommodated by curriculum changes. This was the difference in student characteristics and career goals. Paralleling the diversity of preparation was the difference in their personality characteristics and career goals. The curriculum was unsuited to two types of students: one was the extraordinarily scientifically prepared students, particularly in the quantitative area, who planned careers mainly in research with very little patient care. For these students, the curriculum was not advanced enough and was often repetitious of their college studies. Some schools developed M.D.-Ph.D. programs, but the number of students in these programs was never very large. Second, the curriculum was not suitable for students who planned careers that were biosocially oriented and who shared the characteristics of student-practitioners or student-psychiatrists. For these students, the standard curriculum was too difficult scientifically and the large amounts of basic science at the molecular level was irrelevant to their career goals. It failed to give them the social science and public health courses they required to become family physicians, public health physicians, or psychiatrists.

A multi-tracked curriculum, which would have built on students' preparation, personal characteristics, and career goals would have accommodated all types of students in the pool of applicants whose diverse careers were badly needed by society. Three types of curricula were necessary: 1. A bioquantitative curriculum; 2. The regular bioscientific curriculum; 3. A biosocial curriculum. True, all schools could not afford all three, but each school could have one or two that they could have carried out. These separate curricula would have required separate admissions committees so that students appropriate for each curricula could be selected. This was not done and a golden opportunity, to accommodate the diversity of students and obtain balance in the type of physicians graduated so that society's need for diverse types of physicians could be met, was lost.

Teaching in Medical School

The quality of teaching in medical school declined as faculty attention shifted to research. In 15 years of studies of medical students, there has never been a senior class that did not overwhelmingly state, usually 90%, that teaching in the medical school was poor as compared to what they had experienced in college.

Teaching in the preclinical years was wedded to lectures which were given by many and frequently were of poor caliber. In the clinical years, it was left to overworked house officers who often had only a minimal interest in pedagogy. With their heavy burden of patient care, they were even more exhausted and pressed for time than professors.

No effort was made to tailor the teaching to the needs of the individual student. Close contact with professors could only be obtained by working on a research project with them. Medical schools were reluctant to seek the help of consultants in education, and little use was made of computers, television, or other new learning tools.

Remedial Work

Medical schools, in general, were not receptive to the idea of offering remedial help to students with academic difficulties. The prevailing attitude was that if a student had difficulty, it was the student's fault. If he lacked certain basic skills that would enable him to succeed, it was not the function of the medical school to provide those skills. During the early 1960's, approximately 5% of Harvard medical students had reading problems that interfered with their covering the vast amount of assigned material. Once they received help, they usually succeeded. Having seen large numbers of students who failed out of other medical schools, I frequently found that a lack of reading skills is an underlying factor. Other students had deficiencies in study skills; still others in mathematics. Many schools appointed deans of students to help students with personal problems, but in general, such deans were unfamiliar with what could be accomplished by remedial work, professional counseling, and psychiatric help.

Financing a Medical Education

Financing a medical education during the Scientific Era was not difficult because the financial background of the students was relatively affluent, inflation had not begun to take its toll, and loans and scholarships were adequate.[6]

Such were the dominant characteristics of medical schools as they had developed by 1968. Since that year the pool of applicants from the white majority has not only increased but has included more individuals who formerly would have become applicants for the Ph.D. programs in the sciences. As job prospects for Ph.D.'s have become less sure, college majors with an interest in science have turned increasingly toward medical schools; and even the number of graduate students who have elected to take the MCAT has increased. Medical schools can thus choose among applicants even more academically qualified in science, as reflected in higher grade point averages and MCAT scores.

It is small wonder that most medical faculties, heavily science-oriented by the late 1960s and confronted by increasing numbers of applicants highly qualified in science, should be little interested in recruiting and should regard admissions as a problem in rejecting even qualified students. It is understandable, after the removal of all legal barriers for admission as a result of court decisions in the 1950s and civil rights legislation in 1964, that the common response of the medical schools prior to 1968 to the question of why there were not more minority students enrolled was that any fully qualified minority applicant who could meet the competition for admission would not be discriminated against. If the numbers of minorities were small, it was because the schools and colleges had not yet developed greater numbers of minority students as competitively qualified applicants to meet the established standards for admission to medical school. When the schools and colleges enlarged the pool of prepared and highly qualified applicants, they would be favorably received by the medical school. This kind of response was also common from higher schools other than medicine.

It was this stance, as noted earlier, that Dr. Roy K. Jarecky in November 1968 described as "receptive passivity" but as beginning to yield in medical schools to "positive action with respect to recruiting and preparing RMG [Racial Minority Groups] students for medicine." It is certainly to the credit of medical schools, which operate in the educational sequence at as advanced and extended a level as any field— and more than most—that they were among the first to recognize the need for actively recruiting minority students at both college and school levels by participation in activities well outside their own walls. Given the very particular circumstances affecting medical schools by 1968 (and even at present), it must be acknowledged that willingness to engage in such efforts required an enormous change of existing attitudes and posture.

Recognition of the need to enter upon this course of positive action is still far from universal in medical schools. Even in schools with a very substantial commitment and a large number of minorities enrolled, there are faculty members who are not convinced that these programs are wise and that desirable standards have been maintained. The more modest in size the program for minorities in a given school, the more likely it is that the number of faculty critics is larger.

In discussion with medical faculty about efforts to increase the number of underrepresented minorities, it is not uncommon to encounter the following attitude expressed by members of the white majority: Why cannot "they" (members of the minorities) be like "us?"; we made it on our merits, why cannot they? It is salutary for those who regard themselves as among the majority of Americans, and are engaged in prestigious occupations, to be more conscious of history and of their family's assimilation. It is also well for them to bear in mind the degree to which they have been influenced, quite apart from matters of native intelligence or aptitude, by their family background and socioeconomic origins in moving into higher reaches of education and more highly rewarded and prestigious occupations. Most Americans cannot go back many generations before they find forebears who were immigrants. We ought to give more careful thought to how "we" made it before reaching conclusions about "them."

Most Americans have benefited in varying degrees from the typically American commitment to widespread educational opportunity. Over the past century and a half this commitment has expressed itself in the increasing availability of schooling to ever higher levels provided through both public and private channels. It has played a major role in making the United States a more open and less status-affected society, in which individuals have a larger measure of opportunity to define and work toward their own career goals with a considerable amount of educational assistance socially provided. But one should not exaggerate the degree to which American educational opportunity has emancipated individuals from the influence of family background and socioeconomic origin. By and large, through the use of educational opportunity Americans may alter their roles in society but rarely with complete freedom—certainly within one generation—from restraints related to family origin.

From 1949 to 1954 the Commission on Human Resources and Advanced Training conducted an extensive study of the population going to college. Its data were developed on such a broad basis as to be related primarily to what could be regarded as the American majority. In its report, Dael Wolfle, the director of the study, stated:

> The occupation of a high school student's father is a good predictor of whether or not he will enter college. The socioeconomic factors which are indicated by the father's occupation begin early to influence a child's educational progress and expectations. In some homes a child finds books, parents who value education, and many other things which point him toward college. He is expected and encouraged to do satisfactory school work and when the time for college arrives financial plans have frequently already been made. He "just naturally" goes to college.

> At the other extreme a child grows up in an atmosphere which is little congenial to school matters and educational ambitions. Since he normally plays with children from similar homes, such academic ambitions as he may entertain receive less support than they would if his playmates were from families which expected their children to go to college. These environmental factors work together to discourage educational ambitions. As the child gets old enough to consider leaving school, financial questions arise. Not only is there less money to pay for further education, there is also frequently positive pressure to get to work in order to add to the family income.

> Granting that there are many exceptions to these contrasted conditions, the statistical fact has been demonstrated many times that the socioeconomic background of the child is related to school retardation, academic grades, age of leaving school, and percentage of youngsters who remain in school to any designated level.

> Both intellectual selection—as evidenced earlier—and socioeconomic selection influence continuation through or dropping out of high school. Both factors continue to operate in determining which high school graduates enroll in college. . . .

> After students get to college, however, there is a change. The influence of socioeconomic differences disappears almost entirely. . . .

> The sons and daughters of farmers are the only important exception. Those who start to college are less likely to get degrees than

are the sons and daughters of men in other types of work. The difference may be due to the handicap of poorer elementary and secondary education. Despite many improvements and much consolidation of rural schools, inadequate facilities and poorly prepared teachers are still too common in rural areas. While children of professional and semiprofessional men have a slight advantage over other groups, once a student has entered college, unless he be a farmer's child, his father's occupation apparently makes little difference in whether or not he receives a college degree.[7]

The socioeconomic factors were significantly related to the question of whether or not a person went to college; the son of a professional father was much more likely to enter college than the son of a laborer. But such differences in socioeconomic background were much less evident among students who entered different fields in college. The students who earned degrees in one field came from almost the same kinds of families as did those who earned degrees in another field:

> Yet there were some exceptions to this generalization: majors in the humanities and arts were more likely than were other students to have fathers in the professional and managerial categories and less likely to have fathers in the skilled trades. Social science majors came with relatively high frequency from homes in which the father was in a managerial position. Engineering students were considerably more likely than most groups to have fathers employed in the skilled trades. So were the earth scientists. Students in applied biology were more likely than were other students to have fathers who were farmers or who were engaged in skilled trades. . . .

> The higher the socioeconomic level of the home, the greater the likelihood that the child will earn a degree in a liberal arts or science field. . . .

And finally, directly related to the interest of this study:

> . . . sons of professional men are more likely than are sons of laborers to enter such vocational fields as law or medicine in which a bachelor's degree in one of the arts or sciences is a frequent preliminary.[8]

In 1970 the Commission on Human Resources and Advanced Education reported the results of its later study:

> Since 1954 there has been a gratifying decrease in the percentage of able young people who fail to enter college. The 1954 report es-

timated that 47 per cent of the top fifth of all high school graduates in the country (measured in terms of rank in high school graduating classes) did not go on to college. Data in Chapter 10 of this report shows that only 15 per cent of the boys and 24 per cent of the girls graduating from high school in the top fifth in terms of academic ability do not go to college immediately. Both figures will drop a few percentage points when account is taken of those who entered college after a delay of a year or two.

If one goes down to the next level, the second fifth of all high school graduates, the comparable decrease was from 56 per cent reported as not entering college in the 1954 report to 27 per cent of the boys and 51 per cent of the girls in the mid 1960's.

Many fewer bright students are stopping their educational careers at the end of high school than were stopping at that point 14 years ago. The relationship between academic ability and the probability that a high school graduate will enter college is greater now than it was at the time of the earlier report.

It is gratifying to be able to report these changes, but they are still serious inequalities associated with socioeconomic level. Among boys in the top fifth of all high school graduates, 91 percent of those who are also in the top fifth in socioeconomic status enter college immediately, while only 69 per cent of the boys of similar ability who come from the bottom fifth of homes in terms of socioeconomic status do so. For girls, the comparable figures are 90 per cent and 52 per cent.

So far, the data have been in terms of high school graduates. A considerable number of young people drop out of school before reaching that stage, and here, too, there is socioeconomic selection. The child of the ghetto is much more likely than the child of suburbia to drop out of school before getting his high school diploma. So is the child brought up in one of the rural pockets of poverty that are scattered across the land.[9]

After pointing out that it is not money alone that spells the difference between the educational achievement of students from different socioeconomic levels but also the attitudes deeply rooted in the home that shape the child's development and determine his educational interests and aspirations, the report continued:

It will take at least a generation, and probably longer, to minimize the educational differences attributable to socioeconomic differences. As an analogue, consider the immigrant from a foreign country. The differences between the culture into which he was born and the one into which he has migrated are clearly evident. Although his children are aware of their parents' first-generation status and can see many differences between their parents and the neighboring families who have been here long, they are, nevertheless, educated and adjusted to American customs and values. And their children are full-fledged Americans. The problems of assimilation are somewhat comparable for the children of the bottom socioeconomic levels: culturally, Scarsdale, New York, is as far from Harlem as it is from many foreign countries. The fact that it will take a generation or more to overcome the educational handicaps of low socioeconomic status should not be permitted to serve as an excuse for delay in pushing ahead of the necessary social, educational, and economic actions. Rather it is reason for getting started as quickly as possible to learn what corrective actions will work most effectively.[10]

The more recent study concluded that socioeconomic status (SES) still exerted a substantial influence on the tendency for a high school graduate to go on to college; but, unlike the earlier study, it concluded that socioeconomic status continues to exert some influence on progress in college and even on entry into graduate school:

> Socioeconomic background variables also exerted an independent effect, roughly one-half to three-fourths as great as the influence of academic aptitude, on college attendance and on college progress. Our analysis does not support the idea that socioeconomic influences operate primarily at the point of college entry, and that, once enrolled, the student's progress is primarily determined by ability. While the independent influence of socioeconomic factors was relatively small (partial correlation between .10 and .20 at most educational progress points), the effect of SES at the point of graduate school entry (partial correlation of .12) was almost as large as the relationship (partial correlation of .13) between SES and initial college entry.[11]

The social elevator for individuals provided by educational opportunities may be working for still higher proportions of the American population, but it apparently will take at least a generation, and probably longer, to minimize educational differences attributable to socioeconomic differences.

The making of middle-class America, then, has not been a simple or quick melting-pot operation. It has been a time-consuming, complicated process in which various immigrant groups have had varying histories, affected—whatever the innate potential of individuals—by economic, social, and cultural factors; by prevailing attitudes toward education carried over from the original homeland; by skills brought from the homeland and their compatibility with opportunities for use in the evolving technology of America.

Most immigrant groups started economically at the bottom, whatever their aspirations for a better life. In the nineteenth century there were slums and rural "Appalachias" inhabited by immigrant groups now substantially absorbed into the mainstream of America, but who evidenced the same kinds of social problems now associated with poverty-stricken Black Americans, American Indians, Mexican Americans, or Mainland Puerto Ricans, whether in city ghettos or rural barrios: broken homes, overcrowding, filth and rats, high incidence of disease and infant mortality, abandonment of families, crime, gangs. Cultural differences there are, but not simply as a matter of individual choice. "We," in historical perspective, share more with "them" than is commonly realized or admitted.

Anyone who would think seriously about what are now perceived as the principal minority problems in America, with reference to medicine or for any other purpose, could well start by reading Thomas Sowell's succinct and thought-provoking *Race and Economics.*[12] He provides an illuminating account of later nineteenth- and twentieth-century immigrants (in particular the Jews, Irish, Italians, Japanese Americans, West Indians, Puerto Ricans, and Mexican Americans), comparing ethnic groups in relationship to employment in the market and to government. He also places in broad perspective the particular aspects of black slavery in America, a violent and repressive form of slavery induced by the circumstances of Southern economy and aggravated by its presence within a society avowedly dedicated to freedom and liberty —a circumstance well-described as the American Dilemma. If slavery were to be retained in a society that proclaimed that all men are born free and equal, it could only be reconciled with American social and political ideals by regarding slaves as a special exception, as subhuman beings who had to be defective. A reading of Sowell's book provides at least the beginning of a framework within which medical faculties could view minorities in relation to what is now viewed as the American majority.

It is ironic that in recent decades more efforts have been devoted to equipping Americans to understand culture groups overseas with whom they may have to relate than to equipping majority Americans to understand minority Americans of different cultures resident in enclaves within our frontiers. Beginning in the 1920s, thanks to systematic academic planning centered in the American Council of Learned Societies (later joined by the Social Science Research Council) and to special funding from philanthropic foundations, and more recently from the federal government, colleges and universities extended their capacity to teach and to do research beyond their long-established interest in Western Europe to include the "exotic" languages and cultures of the Near and Middle East, China, Japan, Southeast Asia, Africa, and Latin America. By the 1960s foreign-area study programs were legion, academically highly respectable on most college campuses and vigorously pursued at the research level at many universities. However, as the staff report of the Commission on Human Resources and Advanced Education says, "Culturally, Scarsdale, New York, is as far from Harlem as it is from many foreign countries." [13] Despite this fact, little attention was paid to the culture of minorities resident within the United States.

The appearance of programs in black studies, American Indian studies, and Chicano studies on most campuses in the 1960s came primarily not from conventional academic planning but as a result of pressure from politically active groups, generally minority groups themselves, sometimes supported by white activists. There is no reason why the cultural experience of these minority groups should not be a legitimate subject of study, not only by those whose inheritance is from these cultures but also by white majority Americans who have practical reasons for acquiring some familiarity with the cultural inheritance of minority Americans with whom they share this country. While political turmoil has accompanied the appearance of these minority studies on many campuses, every effort should be made to nurture and guide them toward wide acceptability as valuable programs for minority and majority persons alike. White Americans in general need to know more about the culture and background of their fellow Americans— black, Indian, Mexican American, and Puerto Rican—to understand them better and to work with them. Among others, so do medical faculties.

The incorporation of more minorities in predominantly white medical schools—and a happier retention of the students already involved— calls for more than whites learning about "the other fellow." It calls also for whites learning more about themselves, about their own attitudes concerning racism and the consequences that flow from their dominant imprint upon the situation of the medical school. This kind of learning may indeed be more difficult than "objective" learning about the cultural, social, and psychological characteristics of "the other fellow." Certainly it is likely to be more painfully acquired. I mean the kind of learning that increases one's own self-awareness and awareness of the consequences of one's own values and behavior, not only in terms of direct interpersonal contact but also in terms of the impact upon others of institutional forms maintained by one as a member of a group, particularly a dominant group. This is the kind of learning that can help us deal with racism in our own lives as well as the lives of others. It is a matter of historical record that the American society is pervaded by a strong legacy of racism. We live in that society, and our personality, beliefs, and status have inevitably been influenced by its currents and crosscurrents, including racist attitudes and practices. A measure of self-study may enable us to discover in ourselves even previously unsuspected personal racist attitudes absorbed from the environment; we can then directly confront our own conscious racism, evaluate it, and do with it what we will. This same kind of humanistic and social learning can help us discover our own participation in institutional practices, the effect of which, intended or unintended, as much as personal racism, is to deny or limit true freedom of opportunity to members of minority groups.

This matter of institutional racism and its consequences is far too little understood, as William Sedlacek says:

> Racism may take many forms and stems from the consequences of the actions and feelings of individuals and social institutions. It is important to focus on effects rather than intentions when discussing racism. . . . If we define racism as the negative outcomes that befall a person because they are a member of a certain identifiable group (e.g., blacks) even though we may not have intended it that way, we have a better chance of understanding the phenomenon. For example, a well intended admissions committee which is using inappropriate predictors to select minority students is committing an unconscious act of racism. It is racism because it results in negative outcomes for minority students who are incorrectly selected, and it is institutional racism because it is the result of collective action. Thus, we need not have a raving bigot to have racism.[14]

In the light of such new learning about oneself and the consequences of one's present behavior, one may then decide to alter one's personal racist attitudes and one's form of participation in institutional racist practices.

Let us explore this matter in the context of medical schools, in which it is commonly recognized that most minority students, despite differences in prior experience, encounter culture shock in varying amounts upon entering a predominantly white medical school. The degree to which medical schools provide supporting services to overcome this shock varies from much to little.

There is a general expectation that it is for the student to make the adjustment. Many white medical faculty, however, have found relationships with minority students difficult, and some confess to being troubled by failure to understand various aspects of their behavior. Indeed, white faculty themselves experience their own culture shock when thrown into association with individuals from minority groups with whom they have had little previous contact and whose behavior they find unexpectedly strange. Indeed, minority members often have difficulty relating to and understanding majority members—but the same is obviously true in reverse.

I have found little trace of any effort to study systematically the attitudes and reactions of white majority faculty in relation to minority students. It is easy to understand why. The subject of minority-majority, student-faculty relationships is still too full of stress and pain for all parties to be openly faced by probing research.

The only attempt to conduct such an organized study of which I am aware, in this instance focused on black-white relationships, was made in 1972–74 at the University of Michigan Medical School, which entered the phase of positive action for minorities in 1967 and continues to have one of the nation's largest minority enrollments. A report has not been distributed, although some of its data were used by one of those associated with the research, George Marvin Neely, in his doctoral dissertation in psychology. In a preface to the dissertation, Bruce Gibb of the study staff described the assumptions that inspired the Michigan study:

> Most studies of educational institutions assume that student success depends upon student personality variables. Failure, subsequently, is blamed on the student. Critics of educational institutions tend to blame "the system" and assume that student behavior is a minor determinant of success. The operating assumption for this study is that student performance is determined *both* by the educational environment (peer behavior, course content, teaching methods,

policies regarding student involvement, etc.) and the student characteristics and abilities.

We assume that individual behavior perceived by black students as racist is frequently supported by policies and practices in the medical school even though such support may not be overt.

The study has as an underlying premise that supportive programs and institutional conditions at the medical school as they affect black students can be improved.[15]

The study staff sent questionnaires to all medical faculty and to all black students, and to samples of postdoctoral fellows, residents, interns, and white students; the data were analyzed in terms of three major orientations or attitudes regarding race. These had been developed by Dr. Robert W. Terry in the course of his experience in race relations at the Detroit Industrial Mission.[16] They are summarized by Neely as follows:

Terry presents an analysis which provides one of the new sets of clear alternatives Whites have available to them if America is to become an actively anti-racist society. Whites can be Liberal, Conservative, and New Color Conscious. These alternatives refer to the racial orientations through which Whites may view the problem of racism in America. . . .

The New Color Conscious (NCC) person believes that White behavior and institutions are the causes of America's racial problems and that racism is the institutionalization of subjugation and oppression. Since racism is an institutional form which channels rewards primarily to Whites, espouses White ethnocentric cultural standards, has power residing primarily in the hands of Whites, and operates on the basis of policies and practices which favor Whites and perpetuates White racism, the behavior required to eliminate racism which characterizes the NCC orientation focuses on changing Whites. For example, an NCC orientation would challenge the cultural standards which are implicit in the criteria used to evaluate job performance. These criteria are not always job relevant, e.g., dress style and speech patterns for a technical job that does not involve meeting the public or a client system. The goal of the NCC person is creating a collaborative relationship between Blacks and Whites, especially in making decisions to change the institutions of society. The potential outcome of the NCC position is the recognition and affirmation of cultural differences—pluralism or synergism—and the elimination of the negative effects of racism on both Whites and Blacks.

The Liberal analysis of racial problems in America focuses on the assumed inability of Blacks to garner unto themselves the rewards and material possessions which members of White society enjoy. The Liberal assumes Blacks are the problem because they are sociologically sick. The Liberal attempts to "improve" aspects of Black institutions in an attempt to make them similar to their White counterparts. The Liberal believes, for example, that if the Black family, community, and educational system were improved (that is, made to look more like White institutions) America's racial problems would be solved. This analysis leads Liberals to "help" Blacks to improve Black institutions, the ultimate goal of which is assimilation. However, the resultant assimilation is on White terms, with White values as the determining criteria.

The Conservative shares with the Liberal the belief that Blacks are the problem. However, the Conservative thinks that the problem exists because Blacks are inferior to Whites either genetically or due to "disadvantaged" backgrounds (similar to the Liberal). The behavior acted out by the Conservative, which is based on the assumed inherent differences between Blacks and Whites, results in oppression, control, and domination of Blacks and denial of Black culture. The Conservative recognizes his/her superior power position and works to maintain it in its institutional form. The goal of the Conservative is a separation or domination of other racial groups. As Blacks struggle to free themselves of this oppression, it is speculated that the potential outcome of cultural annihilation becomes more probable. . . .

Terry's primary thesis is that, in spite of being born White and raised in a manner which perpetuates racism, it is possible for Whites to identify that racism and move beyond it. He refers to the ongoing debate in the field of philosophical ethics surrounding the issue of values having any type of objective basis versus being based primarily upon individual personal preference. Terry chooses to acknowledge the existence of objectivity tied to a structure of human experience. This means that Whites can objectively evaluate the role of their values, feelings, and behavior related to racism when tied to their own life experience. Terry thinks that the attitudes and behavior of Whites must be changed, both of which are dependent upon an individual's consciousness or racial orientation.[17]

While the percentage will vary, it seems reasonable to suppose that if the faculty, postdoctoral fellows, residents, interns, and students in any medical school were similarly questioned about attitudes on race, one would find present in varying mixes representatives of all three orientations. The mere attempt to conduct such a survey would appear threatening, would surely meet with resistance, and conceivably would accomplish little in reducing racism.

What might be attempted, however, in recognition of the major need for important new insights to help medical faculty learn to deal with very different kinds of students from those to whom they have been accustomed, is a two-part program. One part is humanistic in character, responding to the question "What manner of man am I in my values as revealed in my attitudes toward these ethnic minorities? Is my orientation that of a Conservative Conscious person? Or a Liberal Conscious person, or a New Color Conscious person?" Terry's charitable hypothesis is that, in spite of being born white and raised in a manner that perpetuates racism, it is possible to identify one's form of racism and to elect to move beyond it. But it does not seem to me that we whites are likely to do so unless we gain an understanding of the particular culture of the minorities and of the history of their experience with whites. This understanding should also be sought in terms of some comparative attention to the history of the movement of other ethnic groups into the mainstream of America. With an improved understanding of the history of a succession of underrepresented minorities, such better informed faculty at least may be able to gain a new perspective on their own role as participants in this human drama; they may then be able to learn interpersonal skills helpful in collaborating more easily with the "modern" minorities. This second learning, the active study of minority culture as a clue to patterns of minority behavior, should go hand in hand for whites with the first special learning, humanistic learning about one's own attitudes toward minorities.

Improvement in relations between the majority and minorities of course is affected also by attitudes of the minority students, and they vary—as do those of the whites. On one occasion, at a medical school that has been consistently active in admitting minority students, principally black, I met with a group of racially mixed students, one-third white and two-thirds black. To an unusal extent the conversation opened up so that the blacks commented on the degree of comfort or lack of comfort they felt in relations with the faculty and with white students. One black student, in no uncertain terms and at some length, indicated her feeling that the atmosphere was generally unfriendly, that the faculty was still basically racist and prejudiced against blacks, and that she did not expect any change. She had concluded that she would confine her efforts to working hard to acquire what she came for, an M.D. degree, and to getting away as fast as possible so that she could return home to take care of her own people. Home meant returning to a rather large black enclave in a city. This student's attitude could be regarded as a black version of the white Conservative Conscious person. In this instance, there is no expectation of any real change in a basically hostile black-white relationship, and the desired situation is a separated minority community having minimal contact with whites. But other attitudes were also expressed. Another medical student, who had listened carefully to her colleague's lengthy outpouring with an expression of growing disagreement, finally looked toward her and said cryptically, "We blacks have our own hangups, too." Other black students, in varying degrees, were less hostile, indicating in general that they had uncomfortable encounters but that they had established friendlier relations with individual faculty members or students. Their attitudes would approximate more nearly those of the New Color Conscious white in which the goal is collaboration in a culturally pluralistic society.

One does find a few persons of minority background who could be regarded as similar to the Liberal Conscious white, in that the goal is integration leading to such complete cultural assimilation with whites as to deny their own origin. In extreme form this can lead to the kind of phenomenon described by Frantz Fanon in *Black Skin, White Masks,* with reference to Frenchified blacks from Martinique in whom the adoption of the majority culture is so complete as to deny any inheritance from their origin.[18]

The primary point is that minorities also have to deal with their own racial prejudices, too, if interracial relationships are to be improved. But this does not alter the fact that the white majority is the dominant party; and if change is to be initiated, it is in the nature of things that the white majority must walk the extra mile. Only then is it reasonable to expect minorities cast in a dependent role to be less wary and more forthcoming in relations with majority persons and to participate also in changes of attitude. Majority commitment to change inevitably must be evidenced first by whites.

Unfortunately, the nation presents, as a *New York Times* editorial of November 16, 1975, headlines it, "Fading Commitment." Noting the decline in financial support of civil rights organizations and the failure of the federal government to enforce civil rights legislation, it finds reports from the private sector no more comforting and concludes:

The erosion of the movement of the sixties has been massive. . . .

A group of housing experts reviewing the results of efforts over the last decade and a half to integrate the suburbs with minorities and lower income families recently confessed failure. Many of the economic gains blacks and other minorities made during the sixties are disappearing as the recession burns away the results of special minority employment efforts. Meanwhile, as a result of massive patterns of resettlement, the minority poor are even more isolated in political units which are increasingly less able to provide them with chances to obtain basic human necessities, much less equal opportunity.

The issue of racial justice has slid precipitously down the scale of American priorities as indicated by the diminution in individual and institutional support for civil rights organizations. The decline is also characterized by a growing tendency to ignore the problem.

The sum of all those elements suggests a sharp decrease in the sense that racial injustice in America is still acute and that the eradication of that injustice is important to the entire society. It is clear that that perception has been missing in Washington for the last several years; but the decline in the funding of civil rights organizations demonstrates that to some extent, at least, the country is following Washington's negative leadership. That is bad news for those seriously concerned about the quality of American life.

This fading commitment to the civil rights movement is also reflected in the mood of medical schools in 1975 toward the effort to bring more minorities into medical school and the practice of medicine. As already noted, underrepresented first-year minority medical students increased noticeably in number and also in the proportion of total first-year enrollment from 1968–69 to 1971–72. For the next three years the numbers increased while the proportions increased by only very small amounts. Finally in 1975–76 there was a decline in first-year enrollment for all minorities other than Mainland Puerto Ricans.

There is widespread awareness within medical school faculties of this slowdown and subsequent decrease in minority enrollment, which is interpreted variously according to individual points of view. Eager protagonists of the enlargement of the number of minorities in medicine view this with deep concern, fearing that conservative forces are at work that could cause further fallback and prevent reaching the goal of minority participation at a level at least roughly proportional to the size of the group in the national population. Those with a more conservative orientation who feel that the schools had already gone overboard in admitting minority students less qualified in grade point averages and MCAT scores and destined to become second-rate doctors find more comfort in the thought that standards may again be maintained.[19]

In any case, this does not seem to be the time to panic. Members of admissions committees with more experience in analyzing minority student performance commonly feel that they have learned something since their first efforts at selection of minority students. In the earlier days greater chances were taken with students with relatively lower grade point averages and MCAT scores. While admission committees are still accepting differentials between the scores of minority and majority students, they regard the scores of minority students as still having predictive value within this group as to their relative ability to handle subsequent medical courses. Minority medical students themselves more often recognize that academic preparation and skills are required and are less inclined to back applicants with substantially lower grade point averages and MCAT scores. One has the impression also that the more conservative faculty is now more openly insistent upon what they regard as the maintenance of standards for all than they may have been in the more enthusiastic and egalitarian atmosphere of the late 1960s and early 1970s. Admissions committees seem to be aware of this pressure and are less willing to take the long shots.

There is, however, an encouraging aspect, for one hears frequently that the minority students admitted more recently seem to present fewer traumatic cases of persistent failure. For the largest group, Black Americans, there is evidence that the promotion rate from the first year, which had been distinctly lower than that for the other minorities, had improved from 1971–72 to 1974–75.

In retrospect, the proposal of the Task Force Report of 1970 that U.S. medical schools reach 1,800 entering minority students by 1975–76 may have been an overly optimistic target for a five-year increase, but the total 1975–76 minority first-year enrollment was 1,391, or 9.1 percent of the total first-year enrollment. This is a far cry from the 292 or 2.9 percent figures for 1968–69.

However, the decline from the 1974–75 level (1,473 first-year minority students, or 10.1 percent of the total) gives us pause as to the future. There is another fact to notice. The increase in the number of minorities was dependent on the presence within medical schools of individuals who were personally committed to supporting what under the best of circumstances could only be a monumental change in medical school policies and procedures, and who could provide leadership for change as administrative or committee officers. These pioneering roles are time-consuming—and no less significant—emotionally exhausting because of the tension in dealing with human relationships among persons who are not only strange to one another but also, because of inevitable cultural inheritances, often estranged in various degrees from one another. For anyone cast in such a role, even if his commitment and values remain constant, his energy and freshness for the continued conduct of an exhausting task will at some point run down. I am struck by the number of such pioneering whites and even rarer minority faculty members who have obviously contributed greatly to the substantial changes for minority participation in medicine but who have passed the baton to others and sought a change of role and responsibilities for themselves. One can only be grateful for their services to a needed cause and be sympathetic to their need for a change of pace.

The time will be approaching when the predominantly white medical schools will be able to draw upon the increased numbers of minority graduates for their new faculty and administrators. At the very least they will offer models of success in medical careers to younger minority students and will be a source of interpretation of the minority experience to white medical faculty and students. Active white leadership, however, remains an urgent necessity.

Something more is needed to refuel medical school dedication to the multifaceted activities still required both to maintain and to increase the present level of minority participation in medicine. The surge in interest in recruiting minorities for medicine starting in the late 1960s certainly was fueled by the earlier national wave of concern for civil rights and equalizing of opportunity that affected many segments of American life. It would appear that much of this commitment, then evidenced within medical schools, was engendered by the general environment and was based on a large measure of emotional reaction or intuition. I have frequently heard within medical schools the statement that faculties themselves were not adequately prepared to work with students so very different from the middle-class whites with whom they were so familiar. Even medical administrators and faculty members who actively participated in special efforts for minority students have commented sadly that their efforts were and are misunderstood by minorities and that they could not understand the reactions they received from minorities. On the other hand, minority students themselves repeatedly indicate that they, as well as minority patients, are simply not understood by the white physicians and medical students.

There is little evidence that medical faculties have received either formally organized or informal short-course schooling about minorities, their special backgrounds, and their attitudes or about the impact of racism on the white majority. Faculty members from a number of schools, themselves sympathetic to the effort to introduce more minorities, have spoken of their own quandaries, doubts, and discomforts, lamenting their lack of preparation and that of other faculty, and sometimes even of white students, for the social experience involved in dealing with students so unfamiliar to them.

Even to maintain the present level of minority participation in medicine—much less to increase it—an effort is needed to help medical school faculties to go beyond intuition and emotional response, for whatever they may be worth, to achieve an increased level of awareness of minority cultures and the history of minority-majority interactions. As will be described shortly, medical school leaders during the past few years have developed many useful programs to facilitate minority entry into medicine, but their continuance and their more sensitive use requires a deeper level of understanding of past racial discrimination, its continuing manifestations, and its consequences. Whatever may be attempted in the way of specific programs, their implementation in the period ahead calls for a special emphasis on means to enable medical faculties to acquire more knowledge about human behavior as it is influenced by cultural inheritances and about racial and ethnic discriminatory patterns.

Such orientation will not be easy for medical faculties. Medical schools themselves generally lack the special intellectual resources for understanding the distinctive behavior patterns of persons from minority backgrounds and cultures. Most present members of medical faculties are highly educated in physics, chemistry, and biology, and their orientation places an emphasis on man as an animal to be studied by the methods of "hard" science. Within the last decade, generally under the label of behavioral scientists, a limited range of social scientists, primarily sociologists, psychologists, and anthropologists who emphasize the use of quantitative methods, has been admitted to a growing number of medical school faculties. The rank and file of medical faculty still have a hesitant or doubting attitude toward these newfangled colleagues whose "soft" science is often regarded as of doubtful utility to medicine. Even humanists are beginning to appear here and there, but still more on the periphery and largely in connection with the analysis of ethical involvements in medical situations. In sum, medical school faculties, with very rare exceptions, do not include scholars in those social and humanistic disciplines that concentrate on the study of human cultures. In any case, they do not seem to have been called upon to play a role in facilitating faculty understanding of minority relationships.

Some help in acquiring new understanding and skills might have been sought earlier from individuals in other faculties in the university, if the need for it had been recognized. More is available now than in 1968, and it should be sought. While it is unlikely that an easy prescription can be found quickly, medical faculties dealing with one or more of the underrepresented minorities should seek the help of colleagues in other university faculties in acquiring some knowledge of minority cultures and of means of interaction with minorities.

An obvious start could be made by holding a series of exploratory conferences in which physician faculty members would meet with academic specialists in various aspects of minority languages and cultures. From these conferences, short courses for other medical faculty members could evolve which would help them to increase their understanding of minority behavior and of better means of interaction with minorities. More convenient materials about minority groups could be developed, and no less important, techniques for exploring latent personal and institutional racism in the majority.

Such a pump-priming effort would have its costs and would be facilitated by foundation and government support. On the basis of the experiences of various medical schools in developing positive programs for encouraging the entry of minorities into medicine, one can describe a recommended course of action, a way to go. But the will to go forward must be there. Medical schools are in need now of refurbishing, refueling the will. Emotional fervor fades without the sustaining support of increased rational understanding of minorities and racism, and of the price we all pay by perpetuating alienated and disadvantaged groups within our own society. This kind of learning may not be about medicine as presently perceived, but it is directly relevant to the ability of medical faculties to recruit and educate minority students and above all to their recognition of the need to make the effort to work with such students. Without this additional learning as a spur to faculty commitment, their will to carry forward with a useful range of activities may well be further eroded.

Plans to encourage such a learning enterprise and strengthened commitment within medical schools can develop through the combined efforts of medical faculty leaders and public and private sponsors. In the hope that the will will be reinforced, let us turn to ways of going forward in minority programs.

NOTES

1. "Medical Education in the United States," *Journal of the American Medical Association* 218 (November 1971): 1220, Table 17.

2. "Medical Education . . . 1974–75," 1341, Table 19 (see note 5, Chapter 3).

3. Comparative data appear in Daniel H. Funkenstein, "Implications of the Rapid Social Changes in Universities and Medical Schools for the Education of Future Physicians," *Journal of Medical Education* 43 (April 1968): 433–454.

4. Daniel H. Funkenstein, "The Prediction of the Career Choices of Students at Graduation From Data Collected on Them at Admission and Matriculation to Medical School 1958–74" (Boston: Harvard Medical School, 1974), 9–11.

5. *Ibid.,* pp. 18–22. The material in this unpublished paper with regard to the successive eras supplements and summarizes content including data on Harvard, Colorado, and Vanderbilt medical students in Daniel H. Funkenstein, "Medical Students, Medical Schools, and Society During Three Eras," in *Psychosocial Aspects of Medical Training,* Robert H. Coombs and Clark E. Vincent, eds. (Springfield, Illinois: Charles C. Thomas, 1971): pp. 229–281.

6. Daniel H. Funkenstein, "Advising Minority Group Students Enrolled in Medical School" (presented at the Meeting on the Advising of Minority Group Students Enrolled in Medical School, jointly sponsored by the Josiah Macy, Jr. Foundation and National Medical Fellowships, Inc., New York City, April 24–26, 1972), mimeographed (Boston: Harvard Medical School).

7. Dael L. Wolfle, *America's Resources of Specialized Talent,* The Report of the Commission on Human Resources and Advanced Training (New York: Harper and Brothers, 1954): pp. 158–161.

8. *Ibid.,* pp. 208–210.

9. John K. Folger, Helen S. Astin, and Alan E. Bayer, *Human Resources and Higher Education,* Staff Report of the Commission on Human Resources and Advanced Education (New York: Russell Sage Foundation, 1970): pp. xxiv, xxv.

10. *Ibid.,* p. xxv.

11. *Ibid.,* p. 155.

12. Thomas Sowell, *Race and Economics* (New York: David McKay Company, Inc., 1975).

13. Folger *et al.*, *Human Resources* (see note 9).

14. William E. Sedlacek, "Non-traditional Predictors of Minority Student Success," mimeographed (College Park, Maryland: Cultural Study Center, Office of Minority Student Education, University of Maryland): p. 3.

15. George Marvin Neely, "Racial Orientation as a Predictor of Perceived Organizational Impact," Ph.D. dissertation, University of Michigan, 1976.

16. Robert W. Terry, *For Whites Only* (Grand Rapids, Michigan: Wm. B. Eerdmans Publishing Company, 1970).

17. Neely, "Racial Orientation," pp. 24–27 (see note 15).

18. Frantz Fanon, *Black Skin, White Masks*, C. L. Markmann, trans. (New York: Grove Press, Inc., 1967).

19. Dr. Bernard D. Davis of the Harvard Medical School recently complained about the admission of disadvantaged students "with substandard qualifications" followed by "the erosion of internal standards" so that "trusting patients. . . pay our irresponsibility," and "many faculty members have wondered in recent years whether the stretching of standards has not exceeded what is reasonable." See Bernard D. Davis, "Sounding Board: Academic Standards in Medical Schools," *New England Journal of Medicine* 294 (May 13, 1976): 1118–1119. Robert H. Ebert responded in "Sounding Board: Facts About Minority Students at Harvard Medical School," *ibid.* 294 (June 17, 1976): 1402–1403; followed by numerous comments and a rebuttal by Dr. Davis in "Medical Education and Minority Students," *ibid.* 295 (July 29, 1976): 291–295. The controversy aroused by Dr. Davis' original statement attracted considerable attention in newspapers in Boston, New York, and Washington and received national prominence in "Minority Report Card," *Newsweek* (July 12, 1976): 74.

Chapter 7
Programs for Minorities

In medical schools having an active program supporting the entry into medicine of disadvantaged minorities, one generally finds a dean or succession of deans openly sympathetic to and supportive of the program, above all as perceived by many members of the faculty. There is a good reason why this should be so. Because of the pattern set in medical schools under the pressure of historical circumstances, the conduct of a successful program for minorities requires many alterations in what faculty have come to regard as customary behavior and expectations on their part; for the presence of even a small number of students culturally and visibly different from the standard white majority constitutes an environmental change, a cultural sea change felt to some degree by all faculty.

For a portion of the faculty, the entry of disadvantaged minorities may entail a substantial change in teaching duties and responsibilities, possibly affecting their career development and often representing difficult personal and emotional challenges. Under such circumstances, it is inevitable that faculty will look for signals indicative of the level of understanding and support emanating from the dean's office. The dean himself may or may not appear very active on this front; the visible leadership role may be played by one or more of his subordinate officers. But the faculty will be concerned to know if there is a committed dean backing up his administrative subordinates and faculty who are encountering new and different experiences in their relation with students. Despite the common faculty disparagement of "administration," faculty personally involved in such adventuresome activities need the assurance that the dean is with them and supportive of their efforts.

This is a realistic perception by faculty members, since the dean does indeed have authority of various kinds. Admittedly within limits, he can provide budgetary assistance. He can influence the availability of special staff support and facilities. His roving mandate enables him to initiate staff and committee studies of new problems brought by unfamiliar students with backgrounds strange to the faculty, studies and recommendations that may be helpful to faculty directly involved in teaching and counseling minority students. To varying degrees he can influence the approval and reward system affecting the status of individual faculty members. A dean known by his faculty to be committed to increasing the numbers of minority students and to providing a proficient instructional program for them is then a major asset in developing a successful program for minorities in a medical school.

In the more successful programs one also usually finds a group of faculty members actively committed to efforts on behalf of minorities and willing to confront the cultural and educational differences among students that warrant changes in their own behavior. This committed and actively involved core group is likely to be associated with a larger group of faculty, most of whom at least acquiesce in the presence of a program for minorities.

Then there is the matter of department chairmen. Whereas department chairmen in other university faculties have seen the power of their role subside, especially in the World War II era, from that of the autocratic "headship" to something much closer to that of a temporary *primus inter pares,* department chairmen in medical faculties have retained long terms, substantial power, and prestige more akin to that of *the* professor. While the active leadership of department chairmen in bringing more minorities into medical school is a great advantage, it is not absolutely necessary for forward movement if there is at least acquiescence on the part of a department chairman in permitting alteration of the activities and responsibilities of those faculty members directly involved in instructing and advising minority students. The greatest impact resulting from the entry of disadvantaged minorities into medical schools has of course been felt by the basic science departments because of their major, if not exclusive, involvement with medical students in the earlier years of the curriculum; it is during this time that the major shock of both academic and cultural adjustment occurs. It has been especially helpful then to have basic science department chairmen who are sympathetic to, or at least acquiescent in, the effort to introduce more minorities into the student body.

To endure and grow, a good program for minorities in medical school must rest on a substantial faculty commitment and willing involvement, sympathetic or acquiescent department chairmen, and a supportive dean.

Having embarked on a course intended to facilitate the entry of minorities into medicine, some schools have gone much farther than others both in the range and depth of change from customary practice.

Recruitment

The most widely represented change in medical schools is in their stance toward recruiting applicants, in this instance students from under-represented minorities. Indeed, all 89 medical schools that responded to the Wellington survey reported that they engaged in recruiting activities for minorities. For no other kind of activity directed toward minorities was universal participation claimed by the respondent schools. It was immediately perceived that if more minorities were to be admitted to medical schools, their numbers within the applicant pool would have to be increased. For purposes of recruitment, two kinds of activity have been developed. One is addressed to informing minority students (most of whom have had little contact with health professionals) about the types of careers that exist in health in order to arouse interest in and aspiration toward careers in health professions including medicine. The other is addressed to informing them, as well as their teachers and counselors, about the kind of educational program that they should pursue in high school and college to prepare them to become better qualified applicants for admission to medical schools. By now many medical schools have had experience in conducting such recruiting programs among minority students, not only among college upperclassmen but also among underclassmen and high school students. The latter have a longer lead time to pursue the kind of instruction that will better prepare them for possible admission to medical school.

The problem now is to continue these recruiting activities until the pool of qualified minority applicants is large enough to permit the admission of minority applicants in numbers more nearly commensurate with their proportion in the American population. Many medical schools on an individual basis have carried on recruiting programs addressed especially to those particular minorities in the region of the country they primarily serve. Early cooperative efforts among medical schools in New York, Philadelphia, Chicago, and Los Angeles to recruit minority students in their respective urban areas proved more difficult to maintain and less successful than individual efforts by medical schools.[1] The predominantly black colleges of the South present a special case. They have traditionally drawn black undergraduate students from outside the South as well; some medical schools, especially in the Northeast as well as in the South, have developed recruiting contacts with these Southern black colleges to encourage their students to consider and prepare for application to medical school.

One does hear complaints from faculty and administrators about their harvest from such recruiting efforts. Students whose interest in medicine appears to have been aroused and whose possibilities as a successful medical student appear promising, may not persevere along the pathway to medicine; other interests may intervene, or family or financial obligations may put an end to their preparation for medical school. Even more frustrating to representatives of a medical school who have aroused an interest in medicine in a minority student who perseveres to become a well-qualified applicant, is the case where the student is granted admission to their school only to matriculate at another school. I have heard numerous laments about the loss of such a sure winner to another school, often for reasons of prestige or ability to offer more financial assistance. In one instance several faculty members vehemently expressed their chagrin at the loss to a highly prestigious school of a minority student with a particularly impressive record whom they had carefully advised over a period of several years; they felt particularly aggrieved because they had been stung by the criticism that they had been admitting students with what were regarded as substandard scores. However, another professor at this school who had overcome an obviously disadvantaged minority background and who has labored sympathetically and mightily to assist minority students to improve their qualifications, revealed a more resigned attitude. If one of his minority group can "make it" in this prestigious school, he commented, his success will still redound to the credit of the group and will set a model to guide others.

These disappointments should not obscure the fact that these recruiting efforts have been rewarded by a sizable increase in the applicant pool and in the number of minority students who do succeed in graduating from medical school. However, since the number of underrepresented minorities in the applicant pool and of students admitted to medical school still falls short of approaching their proportion within the general population, these recruiting activities should be continued until this goal is approached. It should be recognized that these external recruiting efforts are not internal activities directly related to the instruction of students within medical schools. They are a source of better qualified student applicants but not always to the school providing the recruiting program and can be phased out as the goal of approximate representation is approached. Therefore, the costs of recruiting efforts incurred by medical schools are especially appropriate for term grants from foundations and from the federal government.

Another form of recruiting is to offer selected minority students an enriching experience that can help to overcome their educational deficiencies, so that more of them may become upgraded, more promising applicants to medical schools. An early program with this intent was the Macy Premedical Post-Baccalaureate Fellowship Program conducted from 1968 to 1972. Graduates for the most part of predominantly black colleges participated in a special summer session at Haverford (later at Oberlin) and were then enrolled for a year in one of seven selective liberal arts colleges for courses in chemistry, biology, mathematics, and English. Of the 72 minority students who completed this course, 66, or 92 percent, were subsequently granted admission to medical school. This group presented an early demonstration that minority students, including particularly those from predominantly black colleges, could become qualified candidates for admission to medical schools. Helpful as this program was in developing qualified candidates for medicine among those who had already received a baccalaureate degree and who had had little opportunity previously to have a sufficiently intensive scientific educational experience while within their college years, resistance to this approach developed among minority students. Regardless of the fact that there are differences in the level of educational preparation offered by colleges, participation in such a postgraduate program was viewed by some as stamping them very publicly with a badge of inferiority because they had already received a college degree.

By the early 1970s the more common approach had become special summer session programs offered to selected undergraduates at the end of their freshman, sophomore, or junior years. These programs are intended to provide general indoctrination about medical careers and health centers, additional instruction in study skills and English, and special courses in science, particularly biology and chemistry. It is generally agreed that they have enabled more minority students to become better qualified candidates for admission to medical school.

Students at predominantly black colleges have also benefited in their preparation for medicine from recruiting efforts to improve their counseling and from the substantial efforts to update the science instruction offered in these schools through special programs for their faculty. Meanwhile, predominantly white four-year colleges have increased access and opportunities for minorities, so that more minority students now graduate from them. However, a new development in the 1960s needs to be considered. In many states there was a great expansion in the number of community colleges, many of which are in urban areas where their low cost and proximity to minority communities made them particularly attractive to minority students. Even though these institutions offer an academic track, there is a tendency to guide minority students toward what are perceived for them as the more practical courses in vocational and technical education, so that they become qualified for more immediate employment. If, despite guidance toward vocational sequences, they insist upon entering the academic track, they may enter the degree-granting college with deficiencies in academic preparation. If not corrected by an intensive experience in such summer sessions, such deficiencies can preclude their becoming viable candidates for admission to medicine.

It is commonly reported by medical schools that although the minority applicant pool and the numbers admitted have recently leveled off, the quality of educational preparation has improved, so that fewer students have serious academic difficulties than was the case in the late 1960s and early 1970s. Summer programs *do* help. Even if both predominantly black and predominantly white colleges are graduating a greater number of better-prepared minority candidates for medical school, there is still a need to provide assistance to minority college students to increase the number eligible for admission to medical education.

Those medical schools with experience in conducting programs oriented toward medicine and related health professions for minority students should continue such programs, particularly with the help of foundation and public funds.

Admissions

Having embarked on a program of positive action, many predominantly white medical schools not only developed recruiting activities to enlarge the pool of minority applicants; many also recognized the need to make changes in admissions. Three-quarters of the schools responding to the Wellington survey indicated they had changed their criteria for admission, while two-thirds had modified their admission procedure.

As to criteria, by the late 1960s medical school admissions had come to be heavily, though not exclusively, influenced by test scores and grade point averages. With many more applicants than places available, and with the number of applicants in the past decade increasing even more rapidly than the places added by the opening of new medical schools or the expansion of old schools, the pressure to fall back on the objective data provided by MCAT scores and grade point averages as criteria for admission was intensified. Even so, after rejecting those applicants whose scores and grades fell below set levels, medical schools took into account biographical elements provided by the applicant's own statement, letters of recommendation, and reports of interviews in making the final judgment. They have not been bound in their selection of students by adherence to strict numerical sequence in scores and grades. As noted in Chapter 4, what medical schools did in essence in the last decade was to modify their admissions criteria by adding to the list of biographical considerations attention to race or ethnic background related in particular to underrepresented minorities.

Concurrent with the effort to bring more minorities into medicine has been a growing dissatisfaction among medical educators with the measures used in the criteria for admission of all students.[2] The reforming movement to find better measures has been spearheaded by the AAMC and is administered through its Division of Educational Measurement and Research. This effort is culminating in changes embodied in what the AAMC calls the Medical College Admissions Assessment Program (MCAAP).

This new program consists of two parts, referred to as cognitive and noncognitive. While it was generally accepted that the MCAT has been a useful predictor of the probabilities of student success in passing courses in the basic sciences, it was also concluded that it had little relevance to the probabilities of student success in clinical clerkships or as physicians. Even as a cognitive test, the MCAT was recognized as limited to content recall, the capacity to store facts and regurgitate them. Intensive review and study on a national scale has resulted in the development of the new MCAT cognitive assessment tests which, it is believed, will enable students to demonstrate (in addition to basic knowledge of biology, chemistry, and physics) two other important skills: analytical skills based on information presented in reading and quantitative formats, and problem-solving skills. Progress has been substantial in the more familiar terrain of cognitive testing, and the new cognitive tests will be available for use in the spring 1977 administration of the MCAT.

Progress by the AAMC in developing a noncognitive assessment system for use by medical school admissions committees is coming more slowly. Seven personal qualities have been identified as particularly relevant to success as a medical student and presumably physician. They are compassion, coping capabilities, decision-making, interprofessional relations, realistic self-appraisal (including positive orientation toward lifelong learning), sensitivity in interpersonal relations, and staying power (physical and motivational). The AAMC has developed a substantial proposal, not yet funded, which would call for collaboration with five research groups to test various testing procedures for eliciting information about the applicant in relation to these qualities: biographical questionnaires, interview questions designed to assess unrehearsed responses, information tests as measures of interests, paper and pencil tests, and situational tests in which an applicant is asked to respond appropriately to a situation that simulates an actual one.

The aim of this complex and monumental effort is to improve the evaluation and selection of medical school candidates by presenting improved and additional information about those qualities and characteristics of applicants that are believed especially relevant to the role of physicians. When available, the materials for eliciting this kind of non-cognitive information would be offered to medical schools for use on a voluntary basis.

A research venture related to the AAMC's interest in noncognitive matters has recently been launched. The Macy Foundation, in November 1976, provided funds to support a proposal submitted by the Johns Hopkins University on behalf of three collaborating sponsors—the Educational Testing Service, the National Board of Medical Examiners, and the Thirteen School Consortium of Medical Schools, whose membership consists of Case Western Reserve University School of Medicine; University of Chicago, Pritzker School of Medicine; Columbia University College of Physicians and Surgeons; Cornell University Medical College; Duke University School of Medicine; Harvard Medical School; Johns Hopkins University School of Medicine; University of Pennsylvania School of Medicine; University of Pittsburgh School of Medicine; Stanford University School of Medicine; Washington University School of Medicine; University of Rochester School of Medicine and Dentistry; and Yale University School of Medicine. The sponsors will undertake a study of personal and human qualities in the selection and subsequent evaluation of medical students. This proposal also reflects the growing concern among the medical profession and the public that current admissions procedures, with their emphasis on academic indices, are incapable of selecting individuals on the basis of such nonacademic characteristics as integrity, emotional stability, initiative, determination, sensitivity to individuals, and concern for human needs. Studies conducted over the past decade show that a doctor's ability to listen attentively and demonstrate empathy for a patient's concerns have a direct effect on his efficiency in gathering information, the remission or precipitation of illness, patient compliance in following treatment, and patient satisfaction. Since a physician's interaction with a patient or lack thereof may influence the course of treatment, the sponsors believe that it is necessary to develop a wide variety of objective tests to measure these interpersonal factors.

As the basis of the study, the Educational Testing Service, the National Board of Medical Examiners, and the Thirteen School Consortium of Medical Schools will develop a series of simulated interview tests to measure human qualities. Among these simulated tests are patient interviews, employer-employee interviews, and guidance counselor sessions. The results will then be measured against more conventional testing devices, such as personality tests, biographical questionnaires, and personal interviews.

The findings of this study will be coordinated with those of a seventeen-month study supported by the Robert Wood Johnson Foundation, which is attempting to develop selection and outcome measures of a doctor's performance in diagnostic problem solving. It is hoped that both studies will make it possible to establish more effective standards by which medical school students can be selected and subsequently evaluated.

The effort to improve the assessment of personal qualities of *all* medical school applicants certainly legitimates the recognition of concurrently paying close attention to the noncognitive characteristics of minority applicants. For many of these applicants, entry into a predominantly white medical school is attended by special strains from culture shock, as they move from a separated community with its own habits of living into a medical school dominated by an unfamiliar white majority with its own special kind of subculture. Though attention should be paid to the personal qualities of all medical school applicants, it is believed that special attention should be paid to detecting those qualities in minority applicants that might suggest a better prognosis for their perseverance and success.

In the beginning, however, admissions committees had to proceed very much on their own, feeling their way largely by trial and error without benefit of any generally accepted wisdom to guide them. The AAMC became the gathering point for discussion of those noncognitive predictors that seemed particularly relevant in selecting minority applicants more likely to succeed in medical school, as suggested by pragmatic experience and such research as could be found. William E. Sedlacek, a participant in these discussions, comments:

There is a considerable amount of recent evidence to indicate that for minority students, many of the traditional predictors are not optimal indicators of how they will perform at a higher level of education. . . . Most of the work in this area has been with black students and on the transition from high school to college.

He describes eight personal qualities that research indicates are associated with black students who remain in school and college and who are more successful academically. He believes that these qualities may also be useful predictors for minority applicants to medical schools.[3] They are here summarized.

1. *Positive Self-Concept:* Confidence, strong feeling of self, ego strength, independence, determination. Students must have these qualities to survive the shock associated with successfully bridging two cultures. Unlike the typical white student, the minority student who will be successful in school is more likely to have some experience in going against the grain, in being atypical.

2. *Understands and Deals With Racism:* The applicant is a realist whose realism is derived from personal experiences. He is committed to the effort to improve the existing system; he is not submissive to existing wrongs, hateful of society, or a cop-out. He asserts that the medical school should fight racism. Minority students who understand racism, who expect it and are prepared to deal with it, and who are aware that social institutions control them in many ways but nevertheless can be altered, are more likely to remain in school, to adjust better to a predominantly white school, and to perform better academically.

3. *Realistic Self-Appraisal:* The applicant recognizes and accepts the possibility that he may have academic deficiencies and is willing to work hard at self-development. He recognizes the need to broaden his individuality. Recognizing that institutional racism does result in inferior education and background deficiencies in many minorities, he is prepared to work to overcome these deficiencies individually or with the school's help and is more likely to remain in school and be a better student.

4. *Prefers Long-Range Goals to Short-Term or Immediate Needs:* The minority student who cannot—or will not—accept long-deferred gratification accompanied by the special adjustments associated with culture shock will have trouble in remaining in medical school as a successful student.

5. *Availability of a Strong Support Person:* Unlike many whites, many minority students do not have the typical props to fall back upon at a troubled moment. Many do not have members in the immediate family

or neighborhood who have been to college—let alone medical school—or who understand the ins and outs of a system that most whites can take for granted. The minority student with at least one strong support person in the background has an improved chance of making the great and very difficult adjustments required in a predominantly white medical school. Though the argument for this predictor is less sure, it seems to be a favoring circumstance.

6. *Successful Leadership Experience:* This quality is commonly regarded as desirable in majority students, but the problem here is to look not for the evidences of leadership characteristic of the white middle class but to those more often represented in minority experience and less likely to appear as entries in application forms. Although minority students may not have shown their leadership qualities in campus activities, they may have done so within minority community or church activities or even as street gang leaders. If the applicant has succeeded in leadership roles in his own cultural setting, he may do so in medical school, though the evidence here is less sure than that for those qualities described above.

7. *Demonstrated Community Service:* This quality is related of course to leadership but transcends it in providing evidence of an interest in and understanding of one's background and a willingness to help and serve one's own people. If a minority student rejects his own background, it is more likely that he will have trouble with his self-concept, his understanding of racism, and his realistic self-appraisal.

8. *Demonstrated Medical Interests:* Minority applicants may have had direct exposure to hospitals, clinics, or doctors' offices and have been engaged in service work related to health; but for many, whether of rural or urban origin, opportunities for such obvious experiences may be minimal. The development of interest in medicine could be based, however, on time spent in talking to a local physician, in providing first aid to the family, in reading books on medicine, or in other, less obvious ways that can be elicited by questioning and that might reveal an applicant who has developed a real interest in medicine.

Attention to these qualities described by Sedlacek is embodied in the analyses of case histories contained in the *Participant's Workbook* [1] for simulated minority admissions exercises conducted since 1973 under the auspices of the AAMC's Office of Minority Affairs in workshops for members of medical school admissions committees. So far, representatives of about thirty medical schools have participated in these exercises.

In essence, however, each medical school still establishes its own criteria in evaluating noncognitive predictors for minority applicants.

While there is no procedure in sight for numerical scoring of these personality predictors such as is used for cognitive predictors, the efforts described above may lead to more effective ways of collecting information from all medical school applicants with regard to the personal qualities identified as important for students. It is hoped that these better means could be applied as well to producing information of special significance in evaluating noncognitive predictors for minority applicants. In connection with its present MCAAP program, the AAMC should investigate the possibility of supplementing its ways of eliciting information from all applicants about noncognitive qualities with ways of learning about particular qualities relevant to significant differences in their cultural backgrounds.

As previously noted, three-quarters of the medical schools responding to the Wellington survey reported that by 1972–73 they had modified their criteria to make possible the selection of more applicants from minority backgrounds. But how many? Each school faced this question. Slightly over one-fourth (27 percent) responded that they had set a stated percentage of minority students as a goal. In some schools such a result was achieved in essence by stating the goal not as a percentage but as a given number within the fixed total for the entering class.

More schools, however, refrained from defining a set percentage or number ahead of time. The actual number or percentage granted admission would emerge each year as the result of a complex of considerations, with the results in numbers subject to more variation from one year to the next.

Beginning with the applicants for entry in the 1970–71 class, admissions committees were able to use the Medical Minority Applicant Registry established by the AAMC. This enabled applicants, if they chose to do so voluntarily, to identify their ethnic or racial origin in the applicant record, so that each medical school could readily identify most minority applicants within its applicant pool. The availability of this information permitted a change in admissions procedure: a separate consideration of minority applicants, who could then be ranked among themselves after evaluation not only of cognitive scores and grades but also of particular qualities believed relevant to their probable success or failure as medical students.

Recognition of the usefulness or even necessity of separate and special evaluation of minority applicants because of their different experience and background encouraged changes in procedures in addition to criteria of admission. Over two-thirds (67 percent) of the medical schools reported in the Wellington survey that by 1972–73 they had modified their admissions procedures. The most common development was the addition of a committee or subcommittee on minority admissions responsible for reviewing rankings, and recommending to the main committee those minority applicants who should be included in the final list of those offered admission.

Two reasons have commonly been presented for involving a special committee for the admission of minorities. One involves competence for the task of evaluating minority students. It is argued that, because of their history of separation from the underrepresented minority groups, most whites are simply inadequately informed about their cultural and educational experience; they are often unable to communicate effectively and realistically with them and hence are less equipped to make judgments about them than are those more familiar with their cultural backgrounds. Hence the minority admissions group should include persons themselves of minority background, who would also have some knowledge of the medical school world that the successful applicant would enter and of its demands.

The standard mix of members of admissions committees was of course drawn from basic science and clinical faculty who were almost invariably white; very few underrepresented minority individuals were faculty members and available for assignment to admission committees. It was necessary, therefore, to look to diverse sources for members of the minority admissions committee. One such source included staff officers of minority origin appointed as administrators to assist in recruiting minority applicants or in advising and counseling minority medical students. Although these individuals rarely, if ever, had received a medical degree, they might have degrees in public administration, social work, psychology, or education and had recently acquired some familiarity with a medical school. Other sources included minority professors from neighboring institutions, usually having a science background; minority physicians practicing in neighboring communities; and minority medical students in their second, third, or fourth year.

In addition to the issue of the competence of members of the minority admissions committee to judge minority applicants, there is also the argument related to the credibility of an essentially white jury for decisions regarding minority applicants. The tension between the white majority and the underrepresented minorities is still sufficiently great to

make minority participation in the admissions process—even if circumstances require calling upon atypical representatives—a political con-
venience if not indeed a necessity. With a larger number of minorities
as medical students and then as interns and residents, the prospect for
appointing more minorities to medical faculties looks better in the years
ahead; and there will be less need to recruit members of the admissions
committee from outside the medical school administration and faculty.

Sixteen percent of the medical schools reported in the Wellington
survey that by 1972–73 minority students were being selected for admission by a different group from that which selected all other students.
In institutions that establish a given number of places for minorities
within the entering class, the filling of these places can easily be assigned
to a separate committee. But most medical schools have preferred to
function with a single admissions committee empowered to select applicants. It may receive advice and recommendations about minority applicants from a separate committee or subcommittee and then make the
final decision as to who is on the accepted alternate lists. From school to
school and from time to time the influence of the special group on the
main committee may vary, probably from the *pro forma* acceptance of a
slate of minority applicants up to a given number to a fresh review of all
applicants—minority and majority—to determine within the main committee who is finally selected. Since 1973, however, the DeFunis case
and similar challenges of reverse discrimination in medical school admissions have encouraged a tendency to vest actual decisions about the
admission of all applicants in one committee.

Again it should be noted that those familiar with the admissions process often report that admissions committees, including minority admissions subcommittees, have learned to make better judgments about the
prospects of minority applicants. I have been told by minority physicians
from the community and by minority medical students with experience
on admissions committees that they recognize medical school to be a
difficult challenge and that little is to be gained by admitting a minority
student—or any student—with poor prospects of success. While disadvantaged minority applicants may still have educational deficiencies to
overcome after admission, experienced members of minority admissions
committees recognize that the applicants must be able to overcome this
deficiency; and they are now less disposed to argue the case for admitting
minority students with substantially lower MCAT scores and grades
than they may have been in the first wave of enthusiasm to recruit and
admit more minority students.

While individual minority students accepted by medical schools may present academic records easily competitive with those of nonminority students, the mean MCAT scores and undergraduate grade point averages of underrepresented minorities as groups are consistently reported to be below those of the white majority. The AAMC has issued this year the results of analysis of data available for the 1973–74 entering class. It was possible to divide accepted applicants into ethnic categories on the basis of voluntary self-description. The four MCAT scores were available for 33 to 50 percent of the groups, and the undergraduate grade point average was available for 35 to 52 percent of the groups. As shown in Table 8, for accepted white applicants the mean scores on the four MCAT tests ranged around 600, and the mean for their total grade point average was 3.43. Closest to the whites were the accepted American Indians, whose mean scores on the MCAT ranged in the mid-500s and whose mean grade point average was 3.16. The Mexican American and Mainland Puerto Rican group were somewhat lower and were closer together; mean MCAT scores for both groups ranged around 500 and slightly above while their mean grade point averages were 3.03 and 3.07. The group at the lowest end, the Black Americans, had mean MCAT scores in the higher 400s and a mean grade point average of 2.79.

With the continuing accumulation of data such as these, in future years it should be possible to determine whether recent efforts to open more predominantly white undergraduate colleges and universities to minorities and to upgrade instruction for minorities are having the desired effect—enabling more minority students to achieve better MCAT scores and grade point averages, thus diminishing the gap between majority and minority student academic credentials.

The special focus on the admission of more minority students to medical schools in recent years has led to increased attention to cultural variation and to racial and ethnic division and to some interesting questions for the admissions process. As previously described, special consideration of minority applicants arose because of the recognition that because of their physical or cultural characteristics certain groups within America generally experienced unequal treatment by the majority and were excluded from full participation in the life of society. With our particular reference, there are four minorities still substantially underrepresented in medicine. Most members of these groups have been disadvantaged in their educational opportunities and so culturally separated from the majority that they do not have access to experiences that would inform them about, or induce them to try to enter, the field of medicine;

TABLE 8

MCAT Scores and Undergraduate College Grades of Accepted Applicants by Self-Description, 1973–74 Entering Class

Self-Description	Mean MCAT scores				Mean undergraduate grade point averages		
	Verbal	Quanti-tative	General Informa-tion	Science	Science*	All Others	Total
White/Caucasian	576	623	571	604	3.43	3.42	3.43
American Indian	549	572	552	547	3.13	3.22	3.16
Mexican American	510	532	515	521	2.96	3.08	3.03
Mainland Puerto Rican	497	530	499	516	3.00	3.15	3.07
Black American	471	489	471	472	2.64	2.94	2.79

* Biology, Chemistry, Physics, Mathematics

Source: W. F. Dubé and D. G. Johnson, "Medical School Applicants, 1973–74, Supplementary Tables" (DSS Report 76–1, Washington: Association of American Medical Colleges, 1976) Table S–6.

112

hence they may not have developed the academic credentials to the level found among majority applicants. Some, however, may still have the potential to succeed in medical school, and therefore special consideration should be given to minority applicants to determine who should be granted acceptance.

However, it can happen that a minority applicant does not wish to be the object of special consideration. If the medical school to which he has applied has a separate minority admissions committee and one or more admissions committees, he may have the option of not being considered by the minority admissions committee. If he chooses, an applicant of minority origin may not respond to the question for self-description of race or ethnic origin on the MCAT questionnaire; if so, his application would not be reviewed by a special minority admissions committee. It is unlikely that there are many such independent-minded individuals, most minority applicants realistically accepting that there have been differences in the kind of educational opportunity available to them and that there may be an advantage to them personally in a review of their application by a special minority admissions group.

Medical school admissions committees have learned to recognize still another variant. In the present status of our society there is a high probability that applicants of black, American Indian, Mexican American, or Mainland Puerto Rican racial or ethnic origin will in fact have a disadvantaged educational background that warrants special consideration for determination of the applicant's potential. However, in those instances in which an individual of minority origin has had a particular family and educational history that has not imposed an educational disadvantage upon him, his case could then be considered among those presented by the majority applicants—and not really as a disadvantaged minority.

It seems highly probable that the greater awareness in educational and cultural backgrounds of these differences between the general white majority and the underrepresented minorities has helped draw greater attention to the possibility that even within the white majority there are pockets of educationally disadvantaged and culturally isolated whites who would benefit from special efforts to recruit individuals for medicine. The classic model is that of the Appalachian whites, isolated in their hollows, remote from access to modern medicine and contemporary standards of medical care, and limited in the range and amount of readily available schooling. Scattered across the country are other areas less celebrated in myths in which rural and small-town populations are somewhat apart from the mainstreams of urbanized middle-class white culture. Among them, medical school admissions committees are finding whites who, relatively speaking, also may be educationally disadvantaged and less oriented toward an early appreciation of the standard requirements for entry into medicine. Some of them too may have the potential to become qualified medical students, and more of them may be willing to provide medical care to small-town and rural patients.

What was first emphasized as a special concern to admit more underrepresented minorities to medical education in many schools has come to be regarded as a special consideration of applicants who, in addition to disadvantaged individuals of minority origin, may also include disadvantaged whites. Greater awareness of the cultural and educational differences among all Americans on the part of those involved in conducting the admissions process is resulting in a greater effort to assure equality of opportunity for *all* disadvantaged persons who may be motivated to seek a career in medicine, whether they be of minority or majority white origin.

Special Support Programs for Minority Students

After Admission to Medical School

A major shift affecting all parties occurs as the recruiting and admitting phase is passed and the medical school student phase is reached. During the recruiting phase the minority undergraduate remains in surroundings with which he has become familiar; he may have developed an interest in and desire for medical education, but medical school is likely to be a visionary thing given only a superficial touch of reality—if at all— through brief visits to a medical center. He may have been shown a medical school by an older minority medical student. He may have participated with other minorities in a special summer program that includes visits to various medical facilities, or he may have been given a summer research job in a medical school laboratory. Even so, he may emerge as a matriculant at a different medical school, which he saw only briefly when invited for interview; or he may not even have seen the school if he was interviewed by a faculty or staff member who came from the school to interview him closer to his home. For most minority students, actual contact with his own medical school is very likely to be brief and cursory prior to matriculation. At that point his surroundings, housing, eating places, social contacts, and the demands placed upon him shift with overwhelming suddenness from familiar to bewilderingly strange.

I doubt that the habitués of an academic medical center fully appreciate what a very special subculture is established therein. Many an establishment middle-class white on entering such a center finds the internal sets and the regular *dramatis personae* exotic and somewhat theatrical in effect. An academic, for example, from arts and sciences, education, business administration, or even engineering in coming from his part of the campus to the health sciences area finds the region certainly different from his own and unfamiliar. The physical setting is enormously varied and complex: classrooms and laboratories of every kind, an infinity of machines and equipment, innumerable bottles with bizarre contents, exhibits of X-ray mysteries, hospital rooms, nursing stations, vivariums, morgues, waiting rooms, clinics, offices, even a plethora of portraits on the walls, and endless corridors—leading where?

Impressive as these settings may be, they are less bewildering to the visitor than the fauna that stalk these chambers and corridors. There is the medical fraternity itself with its own hierarchy: groups of underclass medical students moving from place to place; the upperclass clinical clerks in twos and threes, or a few more; the intern, the resident, the senior resident; the faculty, regular and clinical by rank; the chairmen; and the deans. But their world is interlaced with Ph.D. basic-science faculty as well as with other professional hierarchies—nurses, dentists, pharmacists, and the burgeoning "other health professionals." Innumerable types of technicians in great numbers and of variable prestige are to be seen. Among the regular occupants are volunteers behind desks or counters serving as receptionists, escorting patients, or pushing them in wheelchairs. Other patients or their families, sometimes looking lost, try to find their way as unfamiliar visitors, deciphering as best they can the cabalistic numbers, labels, and directional signs. Amid all this confusing coming and going, orderlies push carts of supine patients, conscious and unconscious, sometimes piped to bottles overhead, sometimes partially encased in massive casts. The cognoscenti find clues in the length of starched white coats or (in surgical areas) in the unstarched green washable uniforms, or in the identification tags that often designate functions in three- or four-syllable words, in addition to names followed by signs for degrees and certifications that are also mysteries to most people. For the uninitiated these visible trappings only add to the quality of strangeness of the medical center. That a medical center and its denizens provide the exotic background and cast of characters that are the stuff of drama for many people is amply demonstrated by TV programming.

Even for middle-class white students, advancing from college to the medical school in the same university is something of a jump into a new world. But since it is more likely that such students will have ready access to standard medical care, they may have been exposed to clinics or even hospitalization in a medical center. They may also have physicians in the family or among their friends, or be familiar with health professionals in their neighborhoods who can provide almost by osmosis some introduction to this medical school culture. Through the intervention of family and friends there may also be forthcoming on their arrival at medical school social contacts with members of the faculty or house staff who can informally become mentors, guides, and interpreters. Since they are white and medical school personnel are predominantly white, it follows that the environment, even if somewhat new and different, is not totally alien to the white matriculants.

For most minority students, however, admission to medical school means entrance into a strange social situation that is even more unfamiliar to them. For them as for the white majority, it is also highly competitive, authoritarian, relatively rigid, time-consuming, and demanding of single-minded dedication to assigned tasks. Of particular significance for minorities, it is also essentially a white Anglo preserve with differences in culture, idiom, or even language, a place in which they are likely to find certainly at the beginning difficulty in easy and frank communication with most of the people around them and to feel as a result emotional tension.

It would be difficult to overemphasize the magnitude of the cultural adjustment, the shock of cultural adjustment faced by many minority students. In conversation after conversation they revealed the painful process by which they had to learn largely on their own how the "system" in medical school works. They were conscious of the advantages enjoyed by white students in having older acquaintances, family or friends, physicians or other health professionals who could clue them in, console, and advise them—and relieve the tension. They noted the easier access of the white students to social mixing with the white faculty or house staff in their homes, on the tennis court, or even in corridor conversation. In these settings clues and interpretations were passed to these fortunate students, whereas minority students generally found it difficult or impossible to achieve such informal relationships with faculty or staff. A third-year Mexican American student, the first in his family to have contact with medical affairs or medical school, remarked that every day brought to light a hitherto unknown aspect and that he doubted that he had yet acquired an understanding of what it would be like to be a physician. In addition to general culture shock, most minority medical students also contend with and must strive to overcome some measure of academic deficiency, at least in their first year.

If the matriculation phase places severe burdens on minority students, it also has a more substantial effect on the faculty. Although a small number of very interested and highly motivated faculty may participate in extramural visits to colleges and schools, describing health careers and medicine to arouse the interest of minority students, much of the responsibility for recruiting contacts with potential minority applicants has been borne by those who are not regular medical faculty members. Some basic science as well as clinical faculty members may also become participants in summer enrichment programs for minority college students. Faculty members participating directly in the admitting process become substantially involved in the issues associated with minority admissions, and through interviews and associated contacts they may have direct relations with minority individuals; but at any given time the number of faculty so involved is not large. Thus, during the extramural phases of recruiting and admitting, direct contact with minorities is confined to a smaller number of the medical faculty.

The intramural phase begins with the matriculation of minority medical students and their continued appearance within the walls of the medical center. At this stage an increasing number of faculty begin to have direct contact with minority persons as medical students now directly involved in their environment. At this stage the general ethos of a larger part of the faculty and administration becomes critical in determining the kind of provisions that will be made by the school for minorities enrolled as students. It is also at this stage that the general ethos of the faculty at large becomes more apparent to minority students and influences more substantially the kind of reaction they will develop toward the school.

It is at the level of support programs for enrolled minority students that one finds more substantial dissimilarities among schools. In some schools the prevailing attitude is that once recruiting efforts have been made and minority students have benefited from special health career and academic enrichment programs in high school or college, and special consideration has been given to them in the admissions process, they should not in fact be treated differently from the other students. Indeed, it may be argued, to do so would stamp them as inferior.

Under particular circumstances this minimal approach may work reasonably well for given schools. Even before special efforts to recruit and admit minorities began in 1968, a few minority students had overcome the odds against them, completed high school and college with records that gained them admission to a predominantly white medical school, and received the M.D. degree without benefit of any special support programs. As the record shows, however, such persons had been persistently few. During the wave of change in the late 1960s, minorities were first given special encouragement to enter undergraduate programs in predominantly white institutions, including highly academically oriented private and public institutions.

By the early 1970s more minority students had developed both substantially improved academic backgrounds, particularly in the sciences demanded of medical school applicants, and also the cultural capacity to survive and pursue their own goals in a predominantly white environment. Among these students one would be likely to find the children of middle-class, professional, or at least more highly educated families; the group would also include offspring of less educated families in lower socioeconomic strata who had substantially overcome whatever deterrents such origins produced. Such minority college graduates who have achieved high academic records at predominantly white prestigious institutions tend to cluster at a small number of medical schools.

A few medical schools have the fortunate combination of prestige, established relationships with select undergraduate colleges that regularly prepare qualified applicants for them, helpful geographic considerations, relative freedom from legal or practical residence restrictions that opens the national pool of applicants to them, and the financial resources to create more favorable student aid packages. Such schools are likely to have a large number of applicants, are able to offer admission to applicants with higher academic records from more prestigious colleges, and receive a higher proportion of acceptances from such applicants. Especially if their offers of admission result in a first-year enrollment of five to ten (or possibly fifteen) minority students, they may draw a particular mix of minority matriculants, most of whom have fewer, if any, academic deficiencies and who have had experience in learning to cope in predominantly white environments. For them there is less need for remedial work in academic subjects, and culture shock is dulled. Most of these students can survive with the existing standard support system for all students, even if there is continuing tension because of attitudes in a racially mixed environment.

The number of these viable minority students within the applicant pool, although still small, may be on the increase. Competition for them, however, is intense among those few institutions able to offer sufficient tangible and intangible advantages to attract a high proportion of them. One gains the impression that—even then—rather limited numbers of such students are actually enrolled in any one of these institutions. An institution that has enrolled such a mix of minority students may elect to provide also some special support academically or psychologically for them, but such provisions are generally regarded as unnecessary. Some administrators and faculty members may consider it evidence of true equality not to have any special support provisions for minorities and even voice disapproval of such action. Be that as it may, medical schools with such a mix of students may find special support programs less necessary. They are still contributing to the education of minorities in medicine, and one can be appreciative of that accomplishment. It is doubtful that there are a dozen medical schools having such a mix of minority students that can adopt the stance of "business as usual for all students enrolled" without a number of minority students encountering serious adjustment problems, academically and culturally, which encourage a negative attitude toward the school.

But theirs is not—and cannot be—a successful model for the majority of medical schools. Most of them are affected by one or another circumstances that limits their ready access to and competitive pull from the entire pool of applicants. They may be restricted by law or policy by the residency status of applicants; they may be less supplied with student aid funds; they may enjoy fewer established patterns of relationships with select undergraduate colleges; and they vary in prestige. An important factor of prestige is age, a favorable criterion obviously not available to the one-fourth of all medical schools established only during the past decade. The majority of medical schools may succeed in attracting some minority students with the academic and psychological capacity to adjust easily and with no need for special support or assistance. But since the number of such students is limited, and many schools lack competitive advantage in obtaining them, the minority student mix in these schools includes more students whom experience has indicated can succeed in graduating but who face greater problems in adjustment and thus can be helped through the provision of special support services.

One needs only visit a number of medical schools and meet minority students to sense immediately the substantial differences among schools in the mix of minority students. In most schools the student mix contains minority students with academic deficiencies to be overcome and with the need to develop the means of coping with an unfamiliar very white environment. The response of the administration and faculty of such schools to this student presence becomes very important. In some schools a willingness evolves to learn new patterns of behavior in teaching, counseling, and social interaction with students of minority background. Faculty adaptability may result in a varied pattern of support services that proves helpful to minority students, increases their level of comfort in association with whites, and makes for a relatively happier relationship to the school. This may and does lead to the happier minority student passing the word to younger minority persons interested in the possibility of medicine that his school is one of the better places. As a consequence this school may not only increase its drawing power for minority students but may even enjoy a competitive advantage in attracting as matriculants a greater number of the more promising students.

In other schools administration and faculty may—and in fact do not—react so sensitively to the presence of minority students still in need of special academic or psychological assistance. With the burden of adaptation thrown upon such students without the provision of special support, a higher incidence of academic difficulty, emotional turmoil, and racial unrest is likely to result.

It is axiomatic that the student is expected to enter school as a learner and to undergo an adjustment process. It is equally axiomatic that the teacher himself is expected to be a learner—certainly about his own subject—undergoing adjustments through a lifelong dedication to keep his knowledge fresh, growing, and up-to-date. But teaching involves not only knowing something but also conveying it to the student. To accomplish this goal, then, a teacher must know something at least about his students. So far as the upper reaches of education, including medical schools, are concerned, learning about students, their attitudes, and behavior is left largely to informal processes of pragmatic experience. Until recently that experience for almost all medical schools has been essentially with the offspring of white middle-class Americans, products of the same cultural background as that of the vast majority of faculty members themselves.

The entry of individuals from the underrepresented minorities presents the faculty with students whose cultural background, idiom, and lifestyle not only differ from those of the white faculty, but are largely unfamiliar to them and are marked by the effects of a history of discriminatory relationships with whites. It would not be unreasonable to suppose that the assumption of responsibility for teaching a wider spectrum of students would imply the necessity of learning about new kinds of students and of effecting certain changes in teaching behavior.

These comments are repeated here because their meaning is still so often ignored. There is no lack of insistence on the need for minority students to adapt and change in order to acquire proficiency in medical education; there is far less emphasis on a commensurate need for teachers to adapt and change to meet the needs of a somewhat different student constituency. The Modern Scientific Era described by Funkenstein has led to a tremendous emphasis in virtually all medical faculties on research in the subject matter of medicine, aided by the availability of research grants and a competitive spirit struggling to advance the science of medicine. It is generally agreed that there has not been a similar emphasis on the teaching obligations of medical faculties. It is not surprising, then, to find a strong current in the direction of faculty expectation of the student's obligation as a learner to adjust to the faculty, with less emphasis on the faculty's adjusting its teaching to students. This is by no means to imply that medical faculties have not adjusted to the presence of underrepresented minorities. It *is* to say that there is a wide spectrum of response by the faculties of medical schools to the question of providing support programs, which was induced by the increased presence of minority students. It is also to say that a substantial number of medical schools should provide more sensitively developed support services for matriculated students that, among other things, are attuned to the particular needs of students from minority backgrounds. A review of such special support activities follows.

Summer Support Programs

In 1975 the AAMC published a special bulletin entitled *Minority Student Opportunities in United States Medical Schools 1975–76,* which contains responses from 108 of the then existing 114 medical schools, 106 of which were predominantly white institutions. Appendix B lists 45 schools (including Howard and Meharry) that offer a special summer program for their new matriculants; so that in effect 43 of the 106 responding predominantly white medical schools offer such programs. One of these, New Mexico, also accepts for its summer program matriculants for schools other than New Mexico. This means that a great majority, 63 of 106, do not offer any of their students an opportunity for an organized preliminary introduction to their first-year program. A number of the medical schools that recently adopted a three-year program for the M.D. degree altered their calendar to begin instruction in July, immediately following the close of the usual academic year. Some of them offer the information in this 1975 report that they cannot include an introductory summer program because of the early start of their first year of instruction. A very large majority of medical schools, however, would not be precluded from offering a special summer program by such a calendar difficulty.

Only half of the 43 predominantly white medical schools with a special summer program make specific reference to minority matriculants in association with such programs. It seems highly probable, however, that most of these programs came into existence in response to the recognition that many newly recruited minority students whom medical schools began to admit in the late 1960s or 1970s would benefit from an organized preliminary indoctrination and remedial or enrichment session before beginning the pressurized first year of medical school. It might then be recognized that certain nonminority matriculants with marginal academic credentials, or some disadvantaged educational history, might also benefit from participation in a summer program. Such a student might also then be invited to attend the session. Hence the institution can say, as a number do, that their summer program is open to majority and minority students—or to any student. Some schools serving a region with an isolated, educationally poorly served rural or small-town population have come to recognize the existence of a distinct constituency of disadvantaged white students, some of whom can be helped toward satisfactory completion of medical education by a remedial or enriching experience in a special summer program.

Participation in special summer programs is generally voluntary. It is not the usual practice to grant admission to medical school conditional upon attendance in the special summer session, though most minority students may be strongly advised or urged to attend. This is a matter that calls for delicate handling. Since a higher proportion of minority students than majority students are more likely to have disadvantaged educational experience, they are also likely to need the benefit of a further enrichment experience. The effort to persuade them to attend a summer session in advance of the regular program is easily read as placing a stamp of inferiority upon them, rather than as a conscientious effort of the school to help them overcome a disadvantage resulting from a real difference in opportunity previously available to them. If the program has been in existence for a couple of years or more, if second- or third-year students look upon their experience in the summer session as helpful—regardless of defects they may have found, and if some of them participate actively with faculty and staff members in planning and manning the program for new students, the risk of a negative response from the new minority students is reduced. This is especially the case if they have been enabled to have some personal contact with the older medical students during or shortly after the admitting process.

The content of these special summer programs varies among institutions. A well-rounded program will contain a number of elements, particularly if those responsible for the program are sensitive to the cultural adjustment as well as the academic needs of the entering students. All programs contain in some form an academic portion, which may include refresher courses in chemistry, physics, and biology; or they may offer a preliminary exposure to one or more of the basic sciences taught in the first year. This instruction may be offered by advanced medical students or graduate students under various degrees of faculty supervision, or by regular faculty. Some schools, however, make an effort to have the students meet and hear as instructors some of the professors who will conduct the courses they will take in the first year. Those schools with an organ systems approach to first-year instruction may arrange selected parts to introduce the students to a mode of instruction that is generally new to them.

Minority students have often had little experience with the multiple-choice, objective testing so commonly used in basic science instruction in medical schools and in the National Medical Board Examinations. Critical decisions about the fate of medical students very often turn on their test scores: passing a course, taking it again, reexamination to determine passing, promotion to the next year or phase, the required passing of National Medical Board Examinations. It is not surprising that examination time is tense for many students—majority as well as minority. In some schools there is an awareness that the scores received on these tests are affected not only by student's knowledge of the science content but also by his knowledge of the kind of English expressions contained therein. Indeed a student may actually know more about the science content than the score reveals because he has in fact failed to understand the English usages peculiar to these tests. In such cases, lack of experience with a rather special kind of English language needs to be overcome before one can really determine what the student does or does not know about the science content, which is the object of the tests. A few schools have sought the help of experts in the field of education or English to provide special tutoring in the art of test-taking itself, an introduction to which may be included in a special summer program. Even if a student is exposed only to drill in a relatively unfamiliar form of testing without the threat of permanent grading, he gains experience that may reduce the emotional pressure when he faces testing that affects his record and status in school.

Exposure to examining procedures may be part of a larger interest in the study skills acquired by students; in this area as well some medical schools turn for assistance to experts elsewhere in the university, particularly in education. Since medical students are exposed to masses of information in notoriously thick textbooks, reading ability and skill in analysis and memorization based on printed material are attributes of the successful student. Reinforcement of these visual learning skills as well as those involved in auditory learning from lectures can be a particular help. Students who will need to memorize a vast new vocabulary of polysyllabic words can be helped by being taught to use even simple devices, such as flash cards.

From interviews I have carried away the impression that medical faculty members who have worked with minority students, especially clinical faculty members, who had formerly emphasized the need for student competence in quantitative thinking and science, have acquired an increased awareness of the importance to a developing physician of verbal skills as well, not only in reading and writing but also in speaking. Hence teaching sessions in English are joined to the sessions on science. Minority students for whom English is a second language, or whose English idiom varies substantially from that of the medical center, can be helped to acquire additional skills in verbal communication by such instructors.

A number of special summer programs include elements intended to introduce students to the medical school environment and to personalities whom the students will subsequently see. While most of the academic sessions have to do with the basic sciences that figure heavily in the opening phase of medical education, there may be lectures or discussion groups with clinicians who talk more about the patient-oriented aspects of medical education. The students may be escorted on visits to the medical center to begin to learn their way through its corridors.

There is also an opportunity to adjust to the sheer change in environment, to determine where one will live and eat, to learn something of the surrounding community. Many first-year minority students at a predominantly white medical school inevitably feel in varying degrees a sense of isolation. Depending upon the characteristics of the school's neighborhood, they may be able during the summer period to establish some contact with minority persons in the surrounding community who may provide some psychological support or relief from whatever pressure the student feels in a predominantly white school environment.

One aspect of summer programs mentioned by minority students is the opportunity, afforded in a smaller group and under less tension than in the regular fall session, to become well acquainted with classmates also of minority origin and with some minority students who have already survived the first year of medical school. Members of such a group can share their findings about the "system" and clues as to its operation; they can give one another psychological support as they meet a strange new environment; and they can begin the habit of studying together to help one another academically, tutoring each other, examining each other.

Still another kind of support person for minority students may emerge out of a summer session. Some schools endeavor to arrange for entering students to have assigned faculty advisors. The resulting relationship may range from infrequent and perfunctory contact to a relationship of some personal meaning to both parties and may prove to be a source of support for the student with regard to academic and even more personal problems. Across color and ethnic barriers it is often difficult to develop meaningful associations between students and a faculty adviser who still is white in most cases. I have been told that a summer session may provide a more favorable opportunity for establishing faculty advisory relationships useful to the student. Faculty members participating in such sessions are often among those more committed to active interest in minority students and are more likely to be outgoing in establishing a personal relationship with a minority student. The more relaxed atmosphere and the smaller group present in a summer session provide a more favorable setting in which to establish a more open student-advisor relationship.

The entering minority medical student who cannot take advantage of a summer introduction to spread these difficult adjustments out over a longer time encounters on the very first day of a rigorously competitive first year a very substantial burden of adjustment. It is not surprising that minority students on the average have more difficulties in the first year than nonminority students. Nor is it surprising that minority students who have had a summer's introduction to medical school not only generally speak positively about this experience for themselves but later in medical school often participate in a highly responsible way in planning and conducting such sessions for their successors.

I believe that a special summer program should be offered for those matriculants who face relatively greater problems of adjustment culturally and academically, certainly many minority students and some majority students. More schools that do not offer a summer program have a mix of minority students for whom the first year would be less traumatic—indeed, in some instances, disastrous—if their students had had the opportunity to participate in a summer's introduction to medical school. I suspect as well that those faculty members and staff who must deal directly with first-year minority students also benefit from their initial exposure to them in the more relaxed and smaller group setting of a special summer session. The problem of social adjustment affects both parties, student and faculty, minority and majority; and the tension in the faculty and staff, as well as in the student, in these first contacts is not quickly or easily overcome. Time is helpful to both, and a special summer program does provide more time for both. More use, then, should be made of summer programs for selected students.

Admittedly there are deterrents to offering summer programs. During the wave of enthusiasm in the last decade for shortening the length of medical education, a few schools, as already noted, went over to a regular three-year program with a possible option to students to extend the program to four years; in 1975–76 there were eleven such schools. Eleven other schools in 1975–76 provided an option for a three- or four-year program. Some, but not all, of these twenty-two schools elected to begin their school years in July and thus eliminated the opportunity for a summer program for their first-year matriculants.

More schools are affected by financial limitations. A special summer program does cost money and may entail an application of faculty and staff time to additional instructional responsibilities. Since a large percent of the matriculants who would benefit from the summer program come from poorer families, there is also a need for summer stipends to maintain students and offset potential summer earnings from employment. There is, then, a real cost to these summer sessions; however, if a higher priority were placed upon such programs by more schools, more funds might be found.

Finally, there is once again the issue of discrimination and reverse discrimination. In at least one instance a medical school that offered a special summer session for minority matriculants did not continue the practice in the face of criticism that it gave minorities a head start, and this was preferential treatment. Ironically, special sessions have also been criticized as having stamped a public badge of inferiority on those who attended them! Once again, one can reiterate that an individual who has previously been disadvantaged in educational opportunities may have an unrealized potential that can become actual, if he is given the opportunity to achieve a level of performance that other more fortunate persons have already achieved. Given unequal opportunities in the past, equity need not mean uniform treatment at every point along the line.

Support in the Basic Science Years

In 1963 the Citizens Commission on Graduate Medical Education commissioned by the American Medical Association began the deliberations that culminated in *The Graduate Education of Physicians* (1966), now often referred to as the Millis Report in reference to the commission's very able chairman, Dr. John S. Millis. Notice the word *graduate* in the title of the commission and of the report. Of the twelve members appointed to the commission, only three were physicians. A general briefing was given for the benefit of the nine laymen members, who were informed that the four-year undergraduate program leading to the M.D. degree had become well-standardized and was generally accepted as satisfactory as the preliminary basis for any kind of medical practice. However, serious policy questions had been raised as to the post-M.D. educational programs for physicians in the internship and residency years. There were some disagreements among medical specialists, but substantial controversies had arisen between medical specialists and general practitioners. Therefore, we were told we need not investigate the M.D. program but, rather, should concentrate on the graduate phase of medical education.

This standard undergraduate medical program was essentially the Flexnerian two-year basic science program of lectures, textbooks, and laboratory exercises, reinforced by the trends associated with the Scientific Era as described by Funkenstein. These departmentally organized courses in anatomy, physiology, biochemistry, microbiology, pathology, and pharmacology were followed by an introduction to clinical medicine and clinical clerkships in the medical specialties.

During this period (1963–66) competition to enter medical school was increasing, with admission heavily affected by grades, especially in science courses, and by MCAT scores with special emphasis on the science section. Though medical school catalogs commonly refer to the desirability for a prospective student of having received a broad undergraduate education, the emphasis on science is loud and clear in the subjects listed as required for admission. The AAMC annual *Medical School Admission Requirements* regularly lists for each entering class "Premedical Subjects Required by U.S. Medical Schools," a table that demonstrates the emphasis on biological sciences and chemistry, followed by physics and mathematics. While a large majority of medical schools also require English, this is more for purposes of developing communication skills than for encouraging humanistic learning. Even though there has been in the last decade much talk and a little action in medical schools about behavioral science content in medical education, only 15 percent of the schools require any preparation in the social and behavioral sciences.

There have been other curricular innovations in medical schools in the past decade. The almost exclusive preoccupation with basic science in the first two years has been altered in various ways to bring the clinical aspects of medicine and patient contact sooner within the purview of students. An introduction to clinical medicine may be offered in the first year. The laying-on of hands may be experienced sooner with a course in physical diagnosis. An effort to bring aspects of basic science more relevant to medicine may be made in an organ systems approach, in which professors of clinical medicine collaborate in teaching with basic science professors. Or the basic science years may be compressed into one year, despite complaints that students lose experience in the laboratory and that too much learning and memorizing is required of them in one congested year.

However their success is measured, these innovations have not diminished the heavy preoccupation with instruction in these basic sciences in the earlier phase of medical school. A high and growing percent of the applicants accepted in recent years not only take the required courses in biology, chemistry, and physics; they go beyond the requirement to major in subjects closely related to biology, chemistry, and physics. *Medical School Admission Requirements* for 1975–76, 1976–77, and 1977–78 provide in the chapter on "Premedical Planning" tables showing the undergraduate majors of accepted applicants for recent entering classes. Students who had majored in biology, chemistry, or physics and variants thereof (premedical, biochemistry, microbiology, chemistry and biology, other biological sciences, physiology, psychobiology, and biomedical engineering) amounted in 1972–73 to 66 percent, in 1973–74, 69 percent, and in 1974–75, 71 percent of the total accepted applicants. From increasing numbers of applicants, then, medical schools have been accepting students, higher and higher percentages of whom have concentrated heavily on science, and who, conscious of the competition for entry, have become competitive for and have achieved high grade point averages and MCAT scores, especially in science. Hence by the late 1960s medical schools were accustomed to receiving entering students who were already well prepared to succeed in passing the basic science courses. Indeed, they have been so well-prepared that complaints are heard of boredom with repetitiveness of the basic science courses in medical school.

Consequently, by the late 1960s an extremely high percent of medical school classes, in the high 90 percentiles, were promoted to the next year or phase of the curriculum. There appeared to be no need for an academic support or assistance program under these circumstances, since students so rarely experienced academic difficulty in the basic science years, and little more than the standard teaching stint was required of a faculty simultaneously exposed to pressures for research. Now and then a student might encounter difficulty detected before the final examination in a course. He might be advised to use the services of a tutor, either a student very successful in his own studies or often a graduate student pursuing a Ph.D. in a basic science department. A faculty member dedicated to teaching responsibilities might provide some review sessions. If such help proved insufficient, and the student failed the course, he might be advised to spend the next summer in a review of the course content prior to taking a makeup examination. He might be required to repeat the whole course, not always easy because of conflicting schedules. Or if the student had the misfortune to fail several courses, he might be required to repeat a whole year's work, thus lengthening the time required to obtain the degree.

Such was the extent of the academic support program in many medical schools in the late 1960s and early 1970s, especially as related to the basic science years in the curriculum. Given the prior academic training, the previously demonstrated level of academic ability, and the competitiveness of the vast majority of students, a minimum tuning of the teaching program to the particular needs of the rare student facing academic difficulty is understandable. It simply was not necessary for the faculty to devote much attention to the student in academic trouble because he appeared so infrequently. Variations in performance did occur—but very infrequently at the level of possible failure.

The deliberate effort in the late 1960s and 1970s to recruit and admit minorities introduced a different kind of student. Many had had a less intense exposure to science than nonminority students. Often they had received it in undergraduate colleges that had not yet been permeated by the "new" biology or other more recent scientific perspectives. Many of these students had grown up in an environment that offered no encouragement to aspire to a career as a physician; if they did so aspire, they were aware of many hurdles in the way. Hence their commitment to scientific study as preparation for medical school may have begun belatedly; and even if potential aptitude had been revealed, their grounding in science may not have reached the level of those long committed to the scientific preparation for medical school entry.

There were also subtle differences in attitudes. Minority students raised in communities turned back upon themselves as a group and denied access to channels for unfettered development as individuals in the majority society, were more community- and less competition-oriented. The nonminority students came from a cultural background strongly influenced by the work ethic of individualistic competitiveness, a value further emphasized by competition for entry into medical school. For nonminority students, a career as a physician appeared feasible if they succeeded in the competition; they could then begin early to prepare themselves to compete for entry. Most nonminority students admitted to medical schools had learned how to compete in the academic game in science and had little need of special assistance from their basic science professors.

Many, though not all, minority students recruited for admission to medical schools pose, on entry, a greater challenge to their professors to cultivate an inadequately developed potential, to advise them on means of overcoming deficiencies remaining from earlier experiences, and of mastering present academic difficulties. The faculties of medical schools vary in the degree of response to this challenge, but to some extent, all of them have been affected by the presence of minority students.

For first-year students who have attended a special summer session many of the program elements that appeared there will be continued in the regular academic year. For students attending medical schools that do not offer a special summer program, these same elements may appear during the regular year. Some schools make available for students detected as needing assistance, instructors in study skills or in the taking of objective examinations. In some schools the whole process of advising students as to their academic progress has been stepped up. Earlier experience with minority students led to the conclusion that in a number of instances too much time had been allowed to pass before a student in difficulty was detected, his academic problems diagnosed, and a regime intended to be helpful was proposed. Some schools initiated especially for the first year more frequent course examinations; some of them were purely diagnostic in their intent to inform the student as well as the school how he was faring and to enable the school to determine if and where special additional study was indicated.

Tutorial assistance has generally been available through the initiative particularly of basic science departments, local autonomy determining who tutors will be, for whom they will be available, whether they will be paid by the school or the student, and what faculty review sessions, if any, will be offered the student. Departments may vary in a given school in the extent to which a student in difficulty is offered assistance. In some schools, however, academic support systems involve considerable coordination among departments and with the dean's office. Each department offering first-year instruction may be requested to designate a faculty member in charge of academic assistance, who will follow the progress of those students receiving special help. These departmental representatives may then meet periodically with an associate dean for student affairs to discuss the academic progress of students in all their courses. Such a conference may lead to the conclusion that a certain student should be advised to reduce his course load—even at the expense of possibly lengthening the time required for the M.D. degree. As I found in my interviews, and as the AMA reported in its December 1975 report on medical education cited in Chapter 3, more and more schools are finding that a number of students who have academic difficulties can overcome them and ultimately graduate if given a chance to follow a decelerated program. Here again, as in advising a student to attend a special summer session, sensitive diplomacy may be required to avoid deep resentment for what was proposed as a step believed to be helpful. If, with or without the benefit of such interim advice, a student reaches the end of the first year and fails to pass a course, he may be given the opportunity to spend the summer in review sessions with tutoring assistance provided preparatory to taking a makeup examination. If he fails a second time, he may be required to repeat the whole course in the ensuing year. If he fails several courses, he may even be required to repeat the entire first year. This is found to be an uncomfortable alternative even if it be necessary in a few cases.

In addition to whatever tutorial or review help may be supplied, it is the common practice for minority students to develop mutual support arrangements. On entry into medical school, with an occasional exception, most minority students tend to associate with one another, in a cluster or clusters to eat together, to engage in social activities together, and to study together. Many administrators and faculties are troubled by what they see in this pattern, namely, a denial of integration and the perpetuation of segregation by the self-segregation of minorities. I share the view of others who are more relaxed about this, accepting such behavior as a necessary stage in a process. All students have ways of forming associations to fulfill their own desires and to share common interests. Minority students entering a predominantly white medical school must spend a considerable time in classes, laboratories, and libraries in association with other students and faculty—the vast majority of whom are white. If they also find it comfortable to draw apart, sharing some time exclusively with those they still strongly feel to be their own kind, sensitivity to their feelings suggests—as a minimum— quiet acceptance of this fact by school authorities.

The road to integration cannot be reached simply by legislative or legal fiat; it must be learned by arduous changes in behavior and feelings that affect all parties to the earlier separation. Part-time clustering of minorities in medical schools is a stage to be expected, to give way only as more minorities and whites are exposed to the *opportunity* to deal with and learn to cope with each other. It is only very recently that minorities and whites in medical schools have encountered this opportunity to any significant degree.

In an honest desire to encourage mixing of minority and majority students, some schools make a special effort to assign places in residence halls, in laboratories, or in study carrels so that minority and majority students are intermingled. This arrangement may be accepted by the students, and some personal associations may occur across racial or ethnic lines; but nonetheless, most minority students still tend to form a cluster or clusters within their own ethnic groups for purposes of eating, social activity, and studying.

Some schools recognize a positive value in clustering at this stage in the entry of minorities into medical schools. As has been noted, sponsors of summer sessions see, as one of the advantages of such sessions, the opportunity for a minority student to form group associations with other minority students before encountering the full pressure of the beginning of the regular year. Similar groups tend to form early in the first year in schools without summer sessions, but they lack the advantage of lead time afforded students offered a summer session opportunity. Such groups are recognized as serving both the cultural and academic adjustments of minority students. Within such groups, minority students, most of whom are less informed about how the "system" works or what is expected of them, can share the harvest of clues gathered by the other members. They can help tutor one another. Particularly as a succession of minority students develops, they can ask for advice, counsel, and even tutoring help from minority students senior to them. And above all they give one another psychological support while each member is meeting the challenges of an unfamiliar environment.

I have been told by junior and senior minority medical students who entered during the first small waves of minority admission of how lonely they felt on arrival. First-year classes tend to be large, and with only one or two others of their group in a large classroom or lecture hall, usually highly visible at that, they felt even more lonely and apart. They envied their younger friends who entered in groups of five or six, or ten or twelve—or even greater numbers. Minority students often referred to the advantages inherent in a group considered to be a "critical mass." I interpreted this as an indication of their being an accepted presence within the class and partly as a matter of increased capacity for mutual help.

Recognizing in varying degrees of formality the existence of such groups, some medical schools collaborate with them for building bridges for more minorities into what have been predominantly white institutions. They may offer advice about, and share in the work of, the recruiting efforts addressed to minority populations. They may be asked to greet and escort potential minority applicants visiting the school. They may play a significant role in planning and staffing the special summer sessions for matriculating students. With the establishment of happy relationships with the school, they may become the best advocates of the school to minority communities.

Some schools also recognize the potential role of such groups in mutual help in academic matters and collaborate with them in advice on tutoring. They may even make available an area that, in addition to serving as a social rallying point, may also be equipped with study aids, course outlines, lecture notes, demonstration materials, self-learning materials, tapes, the requisite audiovisual equipment, and files of old examinations. I have also heard criticism of this practice; but if similar aids are available elsewhere to other students who need them, it seems to me reasonable to accept at this stage the utility of such a halfway house in which minority students feel more comfortable and are better able to apply their minds to learning. It also seems to me wise to accept and to work with such clustering as a stage that reflects the continuing existence of certain cultural differences and emotional feeling that cannot be hurriedly removed but that may eventually yield to greater freedom of movement and association between individuals of minority and nonminority origins.

In the schools establishing a working relationship with minority students as a group, there are potential advantages for minority students—but there is also a risk to be watched by administrators and faculty. The clustering occurs because the students share certain experiences and feelings; but they are, after all, individuals who differ from one another, and each ultimately has his own identity. When their numbers are small and it is quite easy for them to feel that they are few among the many, they are more likely to present a common front. There is then a risk that the administrators and faculty will be led to see these students more as stereotypes than as individuals, and minority students themselves sometimes complain that this occurs. When minority student enrollment reaches larger numbers, twenty or thirty to a class, their individual sense of security seems to increase and the sense of group solidarity gives way to a freer expression of individual reactions to problems as they come along. The minority student, like any other, wants "to be me"—seen and evaluated as an individual, no matter what his associations may be. Even while working with minority students as a group, nonminority administrators and faculty must be on guard not to be limited by stereotyped perceptions.

Curricular Rigidity

The accidents of curricular structure in medical schools have had much to do with the ease or difficulty faced by a school that tries to address the special instructional needs of students with more serious academic difficulties whom it wishes to offer another chance or two to succeed.

The pattern of medical education widely followed by the early 1960s, which served as the background for the National Medical Board Examinations Part I, was a two-year sequence comprising primarily rigidly prescribed lecture and laboratory courses in the basic medical sciences. The student's time was heavily scheduled, and there were very few options for free electives or self-instruction. Students were expected to move in orderly array through a rigid curriculum—and almost all did. A student who fell out of the ranks into serious academic difficulty and failed a course became an untidy element in a regimented system that made his problem difficult to handle. The easiest solution was for him to review the course content with a tutor the ensuing summer and pass a makeup examination. The next, and more difficult, expedient was to allow him to move with his class into the next year, if he could somehow conform to the demands of the second-year schedule while attending as a repeater the course offered to the following first-year class. If the unfortunate student encountered serious problems in more than one course, the only alternative then practically available might well be for him to repeat the entire first year, thus adding at least another year to his medical school education.

Any student encountering such a makeup problem faced not only a major dislocation in his timetable because of the inflexibility of the curriculum. He was also publicly visible as a student in trouble. Unable to proceed in an orderly course-by-course march following an established timetable in company with his classmates, he was clearly estranged from his own flock. The student who encountered academic difficulty therefore suffered doubly through damage to his self-esteem in facing failure, and through embarrassment resulting from public exposure of his failure. Such was the fate of an occasional nonminority student in the 1960s, as I noted previously.

In the late 1960s the standard medical curriculum began to undergo changes. The amount of required work in some schools was reduced, and students were given some time within a less filled schedule to use for electives. Alternate pathways were offered, which tended to diminish the movement of a monolithic class through the same sequence of courses. A very few schools have gone so far as virtually to eliminate any notion of a standard curriculum and length of time for completing the M.D. degree, permitting students to develop an individually tailored program more expressive of their individual interests and emphases.

The school might even grant credit for courses taken before entry and might accept courses taught outside the school by other university faculty as part of the student's program. Hence a student in such a school might complete an M.D. degree in three, four, five, or six years. In such schools the students would not all be marching together in serried ranks. With far more individual movement allowed, a student who encountered academic difficulty might even be able to fit a repeat course into his schedule and not be very visible as having broken ranks or been "untracked." Such a student could not stand out from the crowd, since *every* student pursued his special program within a highly flexible curricular structure and timetable. In such a situation everybody is treated alike, because everybody has access to an individually tailored program.

While such extreme flexibility does occur, it is only rarely present. Many schools still encounter tight scheduling problems within a more uniform program for all. Schools that have recently adopted a required three-year program for the M.D. degree find themselves more confined in making adjustments in schedules for individuals. By 1970 medical schools ranged along a wide spectrum according to their curricular rigidity or flexibility. So far as the early basic science phase of instruction was concerned, more schools tended toward rigidity than toward flexibility.

Medical schools were working within this curricular framework when actively recruited minority students began to appear in increasing numbers within the student body. For a combination of cultural and educational reasons, more of these minority than nonminority students encountered a serious difficulty, especially in the first or second year. If individuals were not to be dismissed outright but to be given another chance to overcome a failure or failures, within the system existing in many schools the only readily available options might be to repeat a course, which often posed difficulties in scheduling, or to repeat a year. In either case the student faced the prospect of a slowdown in his medical career and public exposure as being off the regular track. When it emerged that all (or a substantial portion) of these students were of minority origin, it was—and still is—easy for the school's action to be perceived especially by minorities as motivated by racial or ethnic discrimination. Although recommended for remedial reasons, such action may have seemed marked also by punitive aspects.

Under these circumstances the manner in which the decision is reached and the context within which it is communicated become very significant in determining the credibility of the school's action in the eyes of minorities. It is sometimes helpful to give advance warning to *all* students that this possibility exists and that these actions are intended to give a student another chance. Participation of minority persons in discussion of the procedure and of individual cases becomes important. If no minority regular faculty members are available, minority staff advisers may be sufficiently involved to be convinced of the nature of the intentions of the administrators and faculty committees making the decisive judgments. In turn they may be successful interpreters of the school's intentions to individuals required to repeat course work. A similar function is sometimes performed by minority physicians from the neighborhood who are asked to participate in an advisory role. In some schools decisions of this type, while never comfortable for those involved, have been accepted. In other cases resentment remains and, in some cases, open controversy.

I have the impression that there has been some reduction in inflammatory outbursts over this issue, probably for various reasons. Reportedly, as admissions committees have acquired more experience, they are better able to identify and reject those applicants with such a poor chance of achieving success that they will have to repeat courses and still face failure. More students are aware in advance of the risk that if they encounter serious academic difficulty, they may— short of immediate dismissal—be required to follow a repeat program as a further chance to succeed. With increasing experience more schools may have learned to handle these decisions with greater sensitivity in order to achieve acceptance. Better yet, more schools are learning to modify schedules and to identify early students, minority and sometimes also nonminority, who should be advised and permitted to carry a reduced load while overcoming deficiencies and adjusting to the medical school. With more time for fewer courses, they may avoid failure and later even accelerate their progress. Finally, as the curricula of schools grow more flexible, more chances for makeup opportunities become available, with less embarrassing public exposure.

There is reason to hope that remedial procedures to overcome academic difficulties will be less drastic in effect, less publicly embarrassing, and more acceptable as a well-intentioned opportunity. If so, there will be fewer occasions for medical schools to be charged with racial and ethnic discriminatory behavior in handling students with more serious academic difficulties.

Minority Staff and Faculty

Prior to the beginning of positive recruitment of minority students, the number of minority professors in medical schools was minuscule. As we have seen, in the whole nation minority persons with medical training were few to begin with, and many of them lacked the background in research that conditioned appointments to the regular academic faculty. Minority Ph.D. graduates in the basic sciences of medicine were hardly more numerous, and minority academic administrators of medical schools were virtually nonexistent. When medical schools began initiating recruiting activities, they generally lacked personnel with any intimate knowledge of minority communities. A number of schools found it advantageous, therefore, to appoint staff personnel to help in this role who did not have the credentials for faculty appointments but who had background knowledge of schools and colleges and occasionally some exposure to the health fields. Many have a baccalaureate degree or a master's degree in education, psychology, social welfare, or public administration; a few have a Ph.D. in psychology or some field related to education. In origin these recruiting responsibilities may have involved them primarily in extramural activity leading to the identification in college of potential applicants. They may have been asked to participate in interviews with minority students and frequently to serve as advisers to, or even members of, the subcommittee considering the applications of minority students.

Having matriculated, a medical student becomes the continuing responsibility of the faculty and dean. At this point such minority staff members may have no assigned responsibility toward the minority students and little influence on handling them. This termination of any official relationship may be encouraged by the accidents of administrative organization, particularly in those institutions in which staff developed to interest minority students in various health careers is located in the office of the vice-president for health affairs and not in the office of the dean of the medical school. In such a case there is an improved chance that this special staff will not be asked to participate in matters having to do with the progress and status of minority students. Because these students may have become well acquainted with minority staff members during the recruiting or admitting phase, they may continue to relate on an individual basis to the latter on personal or academic matters that have a bearing on the student's progress. A delicate problem of relationships may then develop between this staff and faculty and academic administrators of the medical school.

Various alternatives are available to medical schools. They may finally establish an open liaison between this staff and the medical school so that it can provide some measure of input about enrolled students to faculty committees and school administrators. They may establish within the medical school an office of minority affairs or appoint an assistant for minority affairs, the minority incumbents of which may not be regular faculty members. They may, however, have a background that makes them useful as counselors to minority students on all matters they bring to them, and as advisers to the faculty, promotion committees, and academic administrators on the handling of minority students.

In occasional instances a medical school may have a regular faculty member of minority origin whose personality and interest makes him or her a natural counselor to minority students and an accepted adviser on minority students to the faculty. This role for a minority faculty member is likely to be arduous, demanding of time and energy, and psychologically wearing. Like members of any other group, not every minority person who happens to be a member of the faculty has the temperament or appeal to the students to play this role. Those who do accept such assignments and who, for reasons of professional advancement try to keep up with their teaching and research responsibilities, are generally overworked. Good long-range personnel policy suggests that they should be relieved of their advisory role after a few years and given a leave for refreshment and an opportunity to return to their regular teaching and research activities.

Given the paucity so far of minority medical faculty members in the basic sciences and clinical fields, medical schools still have to rely on minority staff members who do not have the conventional academic credentials for faculty appointments. The status and influence of these members varies enormously. In some medical schools the attitude toward them and their advice shown by academic administrators and influential faculty members makes it evident that their perspectives, insight, and information are sought and valued. Even the location of the offices for minority affairs staff and the quality of the space occupied by them are read by some observers as indicative of their importance—or lack thereof. There are schools, of course, in which no such minority staff has been appointed and minority students have access only to the dean's advisory office for all students. Given the persistence of problems impeding easy communications between whites and minority groups, it is prudent to establish such minority staff members as advisers and interpreters, at least as a temporary expedient.

Some of the counseling and interpreting function can sometimes be provided by other means. Minority persons with the requisite background in education may be brought into the medical school arena as study skills instructors. I have been told that minority students who come to them for assistance, after establishing rapport, may reveal concerns and tensions related to social adjustments that are in fact a more influential cause of academic difficulty than the lack of study skills. Similarly, medical students generally have access to a psychological counseling center somewhere in the institutional environment; psychologists of minority origin are to be found with some frequency on the staff of such centers. Some minority students find it easier to relate to such a person and to bring their problems there. Again there is the possibility for gaining useful insights into students' problems, academic or otherwise, which may be helpful in guiding the administrators and faculty to constructive resolutions of the difficulties impeding their progress.

Of course no alternative could be as effective—or as ardently desired by minority students—as the presence on medical faculties and in important administrative roles of men and women of minority origin. Time and time again minority students vehemently expressed the feeling, "If only we could see someone like us as a physician and faculty member, someone who proved that he could be given recognition and who could make it, someone who would be a model for us."

As noted, medical schools have hardly had time to be seriously tested as to their willingness to select and retain minority physicians for regular faculty appointments. The number of Black Americans receiving M.D. degrees in 1970 was only 165, 2 percent of all degree recipients that year. From 1955 to 1964 the number had remained constant at 166 a year. With four to six years required for internships and residencies, the actively recruited minority graduates are only now beginning to be eligible for consideration for a faculty appointment. In 1973 only 1.9 percent of active physicians (M.D.) had the teaching of medicine as their major professional activity.[5] That percentage of the 1970 graduating class would amount to slightly more than three Black Americans; the number of graduates available from the other underrepresented minorities would be even less. By 1975 the number of Black American M.D. graduates had almost quadrupled to 638. If the number of Black Americans entering teaching about 1980 approximates the percentage of all M.D.s having as their major activity the teaching of medicine, about 12 Black Americans from the 1975 graduating class will enter medical faculties about 1980. Time will tell how rapidly medical schools will actually increase the number of teachers of minority origin. The numbers will probably exceed those mentioned here, because of the competition among over 100 medical schools; but these figures serve to show that medical schools are restricted in their opportunities to appoint substantial numbers of minority physicians as professors who could serve as role models for minority students. Their opportunities in the years ahead will not expand if minority enrollments remain at the present level or, indeed, decrease.

Meanwhile, the more available alternative for obtaining help in building rapport with medical students will be the use of minority persons educated for special supporting roles. Some medical schools have been imaginative and active in bringing such helpers into their orbit, and more should do so until such time as minority-majority tensions have relaxed.

The Clinical Phase of Medical Education

Among the curricular modifications of recent years has been the earlier inclusion of an introductory course or courses in clinical medicine. This may include some instruction in physical diagnosis and history-taking or in other ways that bring students into direct contact with patients or simulated patients. The majority of medical schools introduce such material into the first year or two of the curriculum. Many, but again not all, medical schools will also include during this opening phase courses concerned with human behavior, under such labels as Social Aspects of Medicine, Behavior of Man, Sociomedical Sciences, Behavioral Science, Behavioral and Social Sciences, more rarely Social Science and Humanities, and—at least in one instance—Humanities.

Despite these innovations, the first year or two still comprises predominantly a curriculum in the basic medical sciences, "the Laboratory Branches" as they were denoted by Abraham Flexner: anatomy, physiology, biochemistry, microbiology, pathology, and pharmacology (along with their subdivisions and offshoots), taught either in disciplinary packages or through the organ systems approach. The beginning medical student, nonminority and minority, finds himself deeply immersed in chemistry, physics, and biology in his pursuit of molecules and cells. This aspect of the world requires of those who would see it an art of abstraction that employs its own appropriate, highly disciplined methods, and its own complex—and generally expensive—tools. This scientific form of education at the level required for entry into medical school has not been equally available in our society to all; nor have inducements to the practical use of it been equally distributed. Minorities in particular have been disadvantaged more often than nonminorities in this respect. Recently, however, minorities have been offered the privilege, assistance, and encouragement to become medical students. As noted, a few go through the predominantly basic science years with distinction; many succeed, but their academic records in these years tend to be skewed more than nonminorities toward the lower end of the scale. While a majority proceeds on time to the next phase, a higher proportion of minority than nonminority students is advised to follow a decelerated program or is required to repeat courses after failure.

These opening years, heavily involved in laboratory sciences, have been a time of troubles for minority medical students, who on the average are less prepared in this form of academic study than the nonminority students. These opening years, which present more of an academic challenge to the minority students, are also their years of entry into the less familiar environment of the medical school and health center. And for many this entry is also into a massively white-dominated society within which there are few minority role models. Since most minority students face an accumulation of challenges calling for many kinds of adjustments, it is hardly surprising that this is for them a particularly troubling time; and as we have seen, many but not all medical schools have endeavored to provide varying degrees of special support to assist them through the earlier phase of their education.

By the time these students pass into the clinically dominated portion of the curriculum, the later two, and in a few cases three, years, the time of troubles for them largely—if not always completely—passes away. Faculty and administrators frequently comment that there seem to be fewer problems associated with minorities in the later years of education for the M.D. degree. There is less consciousness of clustering, of the self-segregation disturbing to so many faculty and administrators, as minority students become more intermingled among nonminority students. Third- and fourth-year minority students themselves give the impression of being more relaxed than their junior colleagues, even though they still may be critical of certain aspects of the faculty and school.

There are various reasons why the level of tension should recede, even if it does not disappear. Time has passed, and with experience the students have learned more about their environment and how to cope with it. In addition to having made various cultural adjustments, they have had time to master a copious vocabulary, to learn to study more productively, and to learn how to take examinations. As they approach and sometimes exceed the academic performance of nonminority students, their self-confidence has grown. In sum, they may be able to handle their academic program and their interrelationships with greater ease.

Another reason why minority students seem to have fewer problems relates to the substantial shift in the medical curriculum as it turns from the phase dominated by the basic sciences to that dominated by clinical clerkships in the major aspects of medical practice. The focus now shifts from laboratory science to disease and the evidence thereof as observed in patients in hospitals and clinics. In his diagnosis, in the determination of treatment, and in the subsequent monitoring of therapy, the student now comes in contact with live, thinking, feeling, acting, reacting human beings.

It is not uncommon to hear of cases of nonminority medical students with brilliant records in preclinical science who encounter trouble in clinical clerkships because of serious difficulty in the human relations that are inevitably involved in handling patients. Many nonminority medical students have a relative advantage over minority students in having achieved a higher level of competence in handling medical science by the end of the basic science years, but many minority students may enter the years of clinical instruction relatively better prepared by experience than many of the nonminority students to see the human reactions of patients. Some of this preparation may be attributable to the fact that minorities who graduated from college tended to find employment in such people-involved services as teaching, school administration, counseling, social work, and government service. Academic preparation for these services usually includes more emphases upon the social sciences and humanities than upon the sciences. With this trend of collegiate educational preparation more common among minorities, some of them admitted to medical schools may be relatively short on preparation in science and may have deficiencies to overcome during the basic science years; but they may also carry into the clinical years the useful legacy of exposure to more study of human behavior.

However much advantage from his formal academic preparation the minority student may bring to bear on the human interaction component of the clinical clerkships, he brings with him informal learning attributable to his minority status in a society with a strong racist tradition and a massive white majority. To the minority man or woman, a white person has an aura and a fact of power attributable to membership in the white majority. The whites have a firm control of professions, jobs, education, government, and the law. Whites have even been a physically dangerous species to minorities. Under these circumstances one does not have to go to school to learn to observe other human beings, to read their reactions, to detect early signs indicating their intentions or attitude, to determine who is a friend and who is a foe, who will give a helping hand and who will shove one aside. A minority person living a marginal existence and dependent upon a member of the majority group for a job, for advancement, for material necessities, or for access to some improvement in living conditions, learns even behind an expressionless mask to have eyes and ears alert to the most subtle signals of human behavior. He cannot afford to take people for granted. Experience teaches him to become a student of human behavior.

On the other hand a person born into and reared in the dominant majority has a more secure position in society. Relatively speaking, his social status and well-being are not constantly threatened, and he can better afford to take people for granted. He does not face the same compulsion to be sensitive to every reaction in other people he encounters. He may be alert to human reactions—or he may not; unlike the minority student, his position in society does not place him under compulsion to become a student of human behavior. And as we have seen, majority students have prepared themselves for success in the competition for admission to medical school by academic studies heavily emphasizing the physical and biological sciences, not the social sciences and humanities. On the average, neither experience nor formal education arouses in majority students the same level of sensitivity to human interactions that one finds in minority students.

No element was more repetitive in my conversations with minority students than their criticism of medical faculty for what they perceived as insensitivity to other human beings. Since the faculties are predominantly white, these criticisms at times carried racial overtones. There were references to the failure of faculty to understand them, to their being treated by the faculty not as individuals but as stereotypes that often reflect racial prejudice; but these observations were often accompanied by comments to the effect that the faculty was insensitive or even harsh in dealing with *all* students. Some minority students reported that the entry into medical school of minority students with their problems was the best thing that had happened to majority students. For these students too, they claimed, "got a break" when the faculty felt forced to provide some means of individualized assistance to minority students facing academic difficulties, assistance that was then extended to majority students confronted by similar problems.

I found confirmation of this from other sources. On my visits to medical schools I routinely asked administrators and faculty what effect the presence of more minority students had had on faculty, students, and curriculum. More often than I had anticipated, I drew a reaction of surprise, an indication that the question had not been thought about. When there was a response, it was often to the effect that their presence had imposed greater burdens and problems on the faculty. In a number of instances administrators and an occasional faculty member reported that as a consequence of the presence of minority students, more attention was paid to individual students, particularly to those encountering academic difficulties, often minority—but sometimes majority—students.

Procedures were regularized, and tutorial arrangements were better organized and made available to more students with academic problems; diagnostic tests were developed to provide early detection of students heading toward academic difficulties; promotion committees met more often to monitor students' progress more systematically. Even the academic advising system for students might be subjected to more careful analysis, with the result that the counseling role might be assumed by faculty members who could become advocates for the individual student. They would then be separate from those charged with actually deciding the status of students, thus eliminating the situation in which the associate dean for student affairs and his colleagues might be expected to serve as counselor, advocate, prosecutor, and judge. There is some validity, then, to the observations of minority students that because of their presence medical schools have been forced to pay more attention to individual students of *any* origin.

Minority students also volunteered comments on what they considered the lack of sensitivity of the faculty to patients and their feelings, the disregard for dignity in every human being. I was told stories often about how a professor as attending physician examined a patient in the presence of residents, interns, and student clerks, pointed to physical signs on the body of the patient—and commented on them and on related laboratory tests as evidences of particular disease states—with no attention paid to the patient's reactions of embarrassment, distress, or fear. The minority students claimed to be more alert to patients' feelings and indeed to be offended by what they regarded as the professor's affront to the feelings and dignity of a patient who was often too dependent and fearful to protest openly or reveal his feelings. Minority students asserted that they were interested in the patient's feelings as well as his symptoms.

Such stories could acquire a racial overtone if the patients being treated were of minority origin, often of lower socioeconomic status and therefore dependent upon public hospitals or public funding of their costs of medical care. Minority students, particularly if the patients were of the same minority, could easily identify with the patients, seeing in this insensitive treatment an expression of racist attitude. But such insensitive behavior was not always read as deliberately racist. One minority student attributed it eloquently to a kind of cultural ignorance, which could have been diminished if the faculty were willing to ask her and her fellow students to explain their behavior patterns and to serve as interpreters; such action by the faculty she obviously regarded as unthinkable. Other comments implied that this insensitivity to the feelings and reactions of patients extended to all patients, not just to minority patients.

I do not construe criticisms of this type as intended by minority students to apply to every clinical professor. I interpret them, rather, as indicating that minority students are often distinctly conscious of their own awareness of patient reactions and by and large regard the physician faculty as being less sensitive to and concerned for the reactions of patients than they are.

I found some confirmation at least of minority student sensitivity to patients and their possession of some skill in human interaction with them in frequent comments of administrators and faculty, who spoke positively about their approach to and acceptance by patients. This judgment was supported by the comment that minority students seem to do better in the clinical years. A few emerge as top students in the clinical rotations, and minority students as a whole in relation to non-minority students move upward in class standing from their relatively lower place in the basic science years.

Minority students' interest in personal interaction is reflected in their comments on the situation of medical students as clinical clerks. They are the lowest level apprentices, powerless in the presence of a hierarchy of authorities. At the top is the attending physician who is also their professor, the ultimate authority and judge of their performance. But he is subject to being influenced in his judgments by the observations of the intervening authorities, the chief resident, the residents, and the intern, all of whom may have more time to observe the clerks than the professor. Indeed, it was reported that the intern may be the most dangerous in the group for the clerks, for he himself has just passed from the rank of powerless clerk to a man with a little authority; therefore, he may now be prone to make much use of it. Minority students, walk warily in his presence!

Fear that racist prejudices may affect judgments of the performance of minority students in clerkships still remains. Some minority students express the wish that the objective type examinations so common in the basic sciences were a more important part of the evaluation system for measuring their performance in clinical rotations. They regard these tests as less subject to the influence of racist attitudes than the more subjective judgments reported by the clinical professors aided by the observations of the house staff.

In general, though, both faculty and minority students themselves report that minority students encounter fewer difficulties and less stress in the later years of the M.D. program. There is some occasional grumbling by faculty members about the maintenance of standards for the M.D. degree. In the last several years, however, the recruited minorities have begun to move into internships and residencies, without any great difficulties emerging so far. The entry of more minorities into the graduate phase of medical education does not seem to be accompanied by the stress and the need for remedial work and special support that has accompanied their recruitment into undergraduate medicine.

Minority Physicians for Minority Communities

In the background of the change in medical schools from the policy of "receptive passivity" to "positive action" to recruit minority students, there was talk not only about equalizing opportunity for all individuals but also about the scarcity of medical care, particularly in minority communities. In connection with the latter the underlying presumption was that minority students recruited for medicine would ultimately return to minority communities to practice medicine and provide better care for "their own people."

In my conversations about minorities in medical schools I found, however, that faculty and administrators rarely brought up the matter of the medical care needs of minority communities in this connection. The closest they came to this subject was speculation as to the kinds of medical practice that minority students themselves would choose. The choice, they characteristically felt, was up to the individual student. This approach, giving minority students freedom of choice to determine the kind of practice they aspire to reach, is consistent with the usual faculty attitude toward all students and with the concept of equalizing opportunity for all. I did not encounter any indication that the administrators or faculty were trying to direct minority medical students toward commitment to any communities or groups. Nor did I find any reaction from minority students that they were being pushed by the faculty toward the goal of medical care for their own kind. As one student put it, he was glad that he was not being "programmed" for practice in his community, though he added that he might decide to return to live and practice in his own community.

It is one thing to say that there is no conscious intent of medical schools to direct minority students toward preparation for practice in minority communities. It is another to recognize that minority students, like all students, are exposed in medical schools and, subsequently, in residencies to particular models of medical care. These examples exert a strong influence on the kinds of medicine they will finally practice and may affect the kinds of patients they will seek. By the 1950s the curriculum of most medical schools had already emphasized preparation for and exposure to medical specialties in secondary care. Increased involvement of medical faculties in research as described by Funkenstein led to an emphasis on preparing an even larger contingent of medical students for careers in academic medicine. This development of the 1960s only intensified the emphasis on medical specialties and subspecialties, as university hospitals became centers for tertiary care of patients suffering from rare or difficult medical problems. Medical schools were—and generally still are—dominated by clinical faculties essentially committed to interests in specialty and subspecialty medicine. With an exception to be discussed shortly, this is the kind of medicine and medical practice and the kind of care situation appropriate to them, secondary and tertiary care facilities, to which minority and nonminority students still are primarily exposed.

When I asked administrators or faculty the question, what effect has the presence of an increased and noticeable number of minority students who have been encouraged to enroll had on the curriculum, I drew a blank. In recent years medical faculties have been exposed to contact with new kinds of students, those from underrepresented and underserved minorities. Contact with these different kinds of students has had some effect on provisions for student advising and academic assistance, and on the procedures for review of their progress. As for curricular objectives, however, I could detect no recognition of any influence on the medical school program. Accepting into the medical school a number of students from the ghetto and the barrio has not itself aroused an interest in the problem of bringing more medical care into the ghetto and the barrio. Providing opportunities for medical education to underrepresented minorities so that they may become physicians is perceived, at least so far, as a different problem from trying to educate physicians to bring improved medical care into underserved minority communities. It may be useful to recognize that these are indeed different problems. It seems clear in any case that to this date medical schools have been more active in contributing solutions to one than to the other.

Admittedly, an indirect contribution to improved medical care for minority communities may emerge if more minorities become physicians and give more of their time than nonminorities to the medical care of minorities. It is too early to tell how much the entry of more minority physicians into medical practice will affect the quality and extent of medical care delivered to minorities.

The answer to this question may be affected by another development. An issue about the medical curriculum has arisen, not with reference to the special needs of minority groups for medical care, but rather with reference to claims of the increasing inadequacy of the kinds of medical care available to many of the majority. Conceivably this issue could be extended as well to the matter of inadequate medical care for minority communities. I refer to the conflict that arose within the medical profession itself in the dispute between the general practitioners and the specialists. This has developed more recently into the effort to reduce the proportion of physicians trained to function as specialists or subspecialists for treatment of acute and rare diseases in secondary or tertiary care centers, and to increase the proportion of primary physicians trained to participate in primary care.

In 1966 two groups sponsored by the AMA but free to present their own conclusions both endorsed board certification of "primary" or "family" physicians, the Citizens Commission on Graduate Medical Education (the Millis Commission) in its report, *The Graduate Education of Physicians;* and the ad hoc Committee on Education for Family Practice (the Willard Committee) in its report, *Meeting the Challenge of Family Practice.* A certifying board for family practice was finally approved by the AMA Council on Medical Education in 1969.

These reports and the ideas expressed in them began to circulate in the later 1960s, when specialists had not only become entrenched in the clinical faculties of medical schools but were further strengthened in their hold on the curriculum by the prestige of scientific research supported by the availability of large funds. Within medical faculties the advocates and converts to the cause for the inclusion of primary physicians along with specialty physicians encountered overt and covert opposition from the entrenched specialists. They cannot offer to interested students the ready-made prestige that goes to the incumbents of established and well-recognized specialist roles, no matter how desirable it may be to develop the new role of primary physician. The task is made more difficult by disputes over the proper way and label for developing primary physicians. Are they to be family physicians? Or is a portion of internal medicine to be recaptured from the subspecialties for general internists who will function as primary physicians? Do obstetricians and pediatricians have a place as primary physicians for certain segments of the population?

I have said enough only to indicate some of the circumstances that have caused medical schools in varying degrees to modify their undergraduate curriculum in clinical instruction and the related pattern of their faculty staffing. The object of this change is to add opportunities for students to learn about the functioning of primary physicians in primary care settings, along with the ample and well-established opportunities to observe specialists in secondary and tertiary care settings. The pace of this change in most schools has been slow.

But pressure for change from outside the medical schools and medical profession is mounting. Expressions of dissatisfaction with the kinds of care available, the absence of physicians with a commitment to or even an education for participation in primary care, and the existence of poorly served segments of the population had already been voiced in 1966, when the Millis Commission and Willard Committee reported their recommendations. In a succession of public hearings severe criticisms of the alleged imbalance have been heard: too many specialists, not enough primary physicians, too many underserved patients. These hearings in turn have led to increasing threats of government interference and to some increase within the ranks of medical educators of proponents for modifications. But these proposed changes in the objectives of medical education have not been accepted and effected quickly enough to appease the external critics. By passing the Health Professions Educational Assistance Act of 1976, Congress has acted so as to place the medical schools—which already face serious financial difficulties—under still heavier pressure to develop more primary physicians. Capitation support from the federal government, a specified amount per student enrolled each year, has become a significant item in the finances of medical schools. The act provides capitation in increasing amounts over the fiscal years 1978, 1979, and 1980 subject to certain conditions. One of these requires that each medical school will have filled both its direct and affiliated residency positions in family practice, general internal medicine, general pediatrics, and obstetrics and gynecology by 35 percent in the academic year 1977–78, 40 percent in 1978–79, and 50 percent in 1979–80. Further pressure to meet requirements is contained in the provisions for an increase in funds for guaranteed loans to students—available only if the school has fulfilled the capitation requirements. The act also provides for the continuance and expansion of scholarship funds to students who agree to enter the National Health Service Corps and to serve for two years in an area determined to have a health manpower shortage by the secretary of health, education and welfare. The responsibilities that these students will face later will largely be in primary care, for which they will need preparation.

While this effort to modify the curriculum arose without any special reference to medical care for minorities, it should ultimately lead to the preparation of physicians equipped to provide better care to underserved minority communities. There is, however, no necessary connection between the emergence from the educational process of a minority physician and his becoming a deliverer of medical care to a minority community. For many other groups, education, higher education, and preparation to become a physician have been roads to upward mobility, away from poverty and continued association with the community from which they came. It will certainly be such a road for individuals from the minorities with which the nation is now concerned. One does find, however, among minority medical students, expressions of concern for the fate of the people whose origins they share and awareness of their needs for better medical care.

Any professional curriculum addresses certain problems and provides opportunities designed to aid the student in acquiring knowledge, habits, and skills believed useful in handling these problems as a service to people. If a minority student does have an interest in the possibility of bringing medical care to the ghetto and barrio, there has been until recently very little in the curricula of most predominantly white medical schools to nurture and serve that interest. In the basic science years the focus is primarily on the human body which, as Flexner wrote, "belongs to the animal world"; and so far as I have detected, the attention given to behavioral or social sciences seldom relates to the special problems of minority communities. In the clinical years minority students have been immersed—along with all students—in the practice of specialists treating patients largely episodically for acute and life-threatening conditions in secondary and tertiary medical centers.

It is only recently that medical schools have developed relationships with community clinics and health maintenance organizations intended to provide primary care for conditions that are chronic or not life-threatening, with referral to specialists in the case of more acute or difficult conditions. Many schools are so situated that there are minority communities in the environs. If the school engages in forays outside the established medical centers for the purpose of seeing, learning about, and serving primary care needs, the faculty and students cannot help but become more familiar with the particularities of various kinds of communities—including minority communities. They will learn firsthand the medical needs of patients, and the opportunities and difficulties attendant on serving them. They cannot help but see a range of problems different from those to which medical educators have been accustomed in the secondary and tertiary care centers. It is to be hoped, then, that they can become more active patricipants in trying to find better ways of serving unmet needs.

In visiting medical schools in 1975 I found some instances in which schools had developed clerkship rotations in primary care institutions. These rotations might not be required; they could be elective. Even when offered, the general atmosphere of the school might not be conducive to encourage the student to pursue an interest in the role of the primary physician. I did, however, encounter an instance in which faculty physicians serve as medical staff in publicly organized neighborhood clinics, some of which serve minority populations. Comments of minority students who had experienced these rotations suggested that they tended to sustain and encourage interest in developing themselves as primary physicians for minority communities.

The minority students who emerge from the educational process as qualified specialists may serve the needs of their patients, whatever their origin. The chances are that they will serve more minority patients than otherwise might have access to the care of specialists. But a substantial part of the problem of meeting the needs of minority communities is at another level: bringing the members of these communities within the orbit of quality medical care by bringing the services of primary physicians more directly to them. These physicians will have to have some awareness of the cultural characteristics, in some cases even the different language, of these communities. They will have to have some rapport with these groups of patients. It may not be necessary for these primary physicians themselves to be of minority origin, but such a background may be helpful. In any case there clearly is a need for more primary physicians willing to participate in efforts to bring primary care services to minority communities. External pressure is now being applied to force medical schools to graduate more primary physicians. It is ardently to be hoped that more schools will develop internally the dedication necessary to find ways to educate physicians to fill this needed role. Medical schools may indeed discover that minority students themselves are a resource to be heard and used as helpers in meeting this challenge.

Beyond Minority and Majority

I cannot close this chapter based so heavily on impressions gained from visits to medical schools without a few words as to a certain personal reaction to these visits. I soon discovered that after a day of visiting, I found myself exhausted—at first, it seemed, unreasonably so. I was surprised at this reaction, because the circumstances of my life have made me something of a hardened veteran of visiting universities both in the United States and abroad. I had regulated my schedule so that travel itself did not seem unduly taxing of physical energy. Meeting strangers was not a novelty to me; far from being a burden, it has generally been a rewarding source of pleasure. My reception at the medical schools was proving courteous to cordial. Yet I found myself feeling what for me seemed unusually exhausted at the end of a day's visiting and interviewing.

At the beginning I could not determine the cause of this exhaustion. Before I began my visits I had wondered how freely and easily the parties involved in the entry of more minority students into medical schools would talk to me. I found that I need not have had a concern on this score. I did find instances where I detected reticence in administrators, faculty, and students both of minority and nonminority origin. But these instances were very infrequent. Their existence did help me recognize candor when I encountered it, which was most of the time. Indeed, I was sometimes surprised at the openness of comments on what were basically personal interrelationships within the school. These comments were often of such a character that they would in all likelihood have been uttered in open meetings either not at all or in very muted tones. I was after all an outsider and not a participant in the life of the school. Such candor indicated a trust in my discretion and in my statement that I would not quote comments attributed to individuals. Only on very rare occasions did I find difficulty in opening channels of communication; and when I found this to be the case, I chose to respect the individual's choice and did not expend energy in trying to continue the conversation.

I gradually realized that my exhaustion resulted from an accumulation of sadness. In time it came to me that this sadness was derived from a repetitive aspect of my round of conversations as I went from one school to the next. What induced this feeling of sadness? It clearly did not fit with anger, although I did hear anger expressed, launched in a variety of directions. But I heard more comments that comported better with yearning, an aspiring to something desired but not yet attained. With this clue I could gradually detect the repetitious situations in which this sense of yearning was expressed.

My conversations were of course primarily with persons who had become identified with minorities in medical schools. In addition to the minority students themselves, they were the faculty members, mostly white, directly involved in recruiting, admitting, counseling, teaching, or tutoring the minority students. And they were the administrators and staff participating in various ways in these same relationships to minority students and in policy decisions affecting them.

From each of these parties came descriptions of episodes that indicated an obstacle to the achievement of a desired end, the separation of individuals from satisfying contact because of the sense of racial and ethnic difference.

It was repeatedly revealed in the comments of minority students in stories about their sense of isolation. They felt different sitting in a class. They passed a professor in the corridor who did not talk easily or banter with them, as he did with the white students. He did not play tennis with them. He did not invite them to his home. He did not call on them in class. He did not see them as individuals.

White faculty and administrators often felt that they were misunderstood. They tried to be friendly but could not reach an easy understanding with the minority students. The latter were difficult and remote. They did not respond to invitations to their offices when they felt the need or desire. Their academic demands, intended to help the student develop his knowledge and skill, were not understood as being for his good. Decisions that the student repeat academic work, take remake examinations, be "untracked" or decelerate, were seen as unfair punishments, rather than as opportunities to overcome a real difficulty.

On either side the same question is implied: why cannot "they" accept me? In this question there are two elements, a sense of being deterred from establishing a different relationship and a desire to overcome that deterrence. A sense of unfulfilled desire does induce the feeling of sadness. Hearing stories from both sides, one wishes he could by some magic bring the separated parties together. With no such quick remedy in sight, the listener can easily feel emotionally exhausted.

The experience does confirm to me how heavily our weight of inherited racial and ethnic prejudice rests upon and afflicts all of us and how difficult it is to overcome, even with an underlying desire on both sides to share experience. This experience can well make one sad. But it can also give one hope. For it shows that in medical schools there are now both minority and majority persons who aspire to something different, to a personal relationship with one another that in James Comer's phrase will reach beyond black and white, beyond minority and majority, by becoming a trusting relationship between individuals who are in open communication.

It appears that the relationship between minority medical students and faculties is improving and that more minority students want it to improve. There is certainly a corps of people, more effective in some medical schools than in others, who do want to transcend differences so that minority individuals can be educated and develop professionally as physicians in a multicultural society. But racist and ethnic prejudice is a two-edged sword, harming each of the groups it separates. It is not easily eradicated. Even if its direct manifestations in conscious and intentional prejudice are removed, it can survive and hurt in the actions imposed by institutional forms supported by unconscious habits. Would it help, then, to ease the path for medical schools to educate those minority students already enrolled, and improve the chances that still more might be recruited if efforts were made in medical schools to study, deliberately and openly, racism and ethnic prejudice as a social phenomenon within themselves? This question deserves consideration.[6]

NOTES

1. Dennis B. Dove, "The Medical Educational Establishment Called to Task," *New Physician* 19 (November 1970): 903–907.

2. Maurice Korman, Robert L. Stubblefield, and Lawrence W. Martin, "Patterns of Success in Medical School and Their Correlates," *Journal of Medical Education* 43 (March 1968): 405–411. James B. Erdmann, Dale E. Mattson, Jack G. Hutton, Jr. and Wimburn L. Wallace, "The Medical College Admission Test: Past, Present, Future," *ibid.* 46 (November 1971): 937–946. Ronald L. Hamberg, August G. Swanson, and Charles W. Dohner, "Perceptions and Usage of Predictive Data for Medical School Admissions,"

ibid. 959–963. John R. Wingard and John W. Williamson, "Grades as Predictors of Physicians' Career Performance: An Evaluative Literature Review," *ibid.* 48 (April 1973): 311–322.

3. William E. Sedlacek, "Non–traditional Predictors" (see note 14, Chapter 6.) Similar material is contained in the recently published book, William E. Sedlacek and Glenwood C. Brooks, Jr., *Racism in American Education: A Model for Change* (Chicago: Nelson-Hall, 1976).

4. Ayres G. D'Costa, Philip Bashook, Paul Elliott, Roy Jarecky, Walter Leavell, Dario Prieto, and William Sedlacek, *Simulated Minority Admissions Exercises: Participant's Workbook* (Washington, D.C.: Association of American Medical Colleges, 1974).

5. G. A. Roback, *Distribution of Physicians in the U.S., 1973* (Chicago: American Medical Association, Center for Health Services Research and Development, 1974), p. 38, Table M.

6. A model for undertaking such a study in social change is proposed in Sedlacek and Brooks, *Racism in American Education* (see note 3).

Index

AAMC. *See* Association of American Medical Colleges
Academic preparation, 21, 26, 67, 72, 74
  See also Premedical education
Academic records, 110-12
Academic support programs, 129-31, 135, 145
Admission committees, 109-10, 137
  minority subcommittees, 109-10
Admission policies, 67, 102-14
  applicants. *See* Applicants
  biographical questionnaire, 103-04
  changes in criteria, 102-09
  color-conscious policies, 45, 57
  committees, 109-10, 137
  compensating for past discrimination, 60
  competition for admission, 45-46, 66, 130
  cultural and educational differences, 112-14
  DeFunis case, 46-61, 110
  disadvantaged applicants, 51-52, 113-14
  disadvantaged whites, 45-48, 113-14
  equal protection clause, 51-52
  factors to be considered, 58-59
  legal problems and issues, 43-62
  MCAT and GPA scores, 91, 102-03, 110-12
  minority students, 26-27, 67, 102-14
  historical background, 69-70
  modified procedures, 102-09
  noncognitive predictors, 103-07
  evaluating, 108
  positive programs, 56-57
  preferential treatment, 46, 51-52, 55-60
  premedical requirements, 20-21, 68, 128
  quota system, 50, 60
  reforms in criteria, 103-09
  rejection of qualified students, 76
  "reverse discrimination," 45, 46-58, 61
  rights of nonminority students, 50-51

selecting students, 27, 57-58, 105-07
  See also Selection of students
  simulated minority admissions exercises, 107-08
  special admission programs, 52-55, 58
  standards for admission, 52
  summer session programs, 101
  underrepresented minorities, 111-13
  U.S. Supreme Court decisions, 58-59
"Affirmative action" programs, 45
  See also Positive action programs
Alevy v. Downstate Medical Center of the State of New York, 55
American Council of Learned Societies, 83
American dilemma, 82
American Hospital Association, 23
American Indians, 6, 82-83
  academic records, 111-12
  color discrimination, 45
  enrollment in medical schools, 29-31
  attrition and retention, 34-38
  first-year classes, 30, 33
  promotion rate, 38-39
  number of M.D. graduates, 40
  programs for, 24
  social problems, 82
  in U.S. population, 33
American majority, 82
  educational opportunities, 78-82
  socioeconomic factors, 78-81
American Medical Association (AMA), 23, 127
  Citizens' Commission on Graduate Medical Education (Millis Commission), 15, 127, 149, 150
American Oriental minority groups, 24
Appalachian whites, 113
Applicants to medical schools
  effect of father's occupation, 78-81
  Minority Medical Applicant Registry, 27, 108
  pool of applicants, 70, 72, 100
  in proportion to population, 100
  selection system, 27
  simulated interview tests, 105
  socioeconomic factors, 78-81
  See also Admission policies

157